The Death of Guy Gibson

The Death of Guy Gibson

Who, or What, Killed the Dambuster VC

M.S. Morgan

AIR WORLD

First published in Great Britain in 2024 by
Air World Books
An imprint of
Pen & Sword Books Ltd
Yorkshire - Philadelphia

ISBN: 978 1 03611 937 9

A CIP catalogue record for this book is available from the British Library

Typeset in INDIA by IMPEC eSolutions
Printed and bound in the England by CPI Group (UK) Ltd, Croydon CR0 4YY

Pen & Sword Books Ltd incorporates the imprints of Pen & Sword Archaeology, Air World Books, Atlas, Aviation, Battleground, Discovery, Family History, History, Maritime, Military, Naval, Politics, Social History, Transport, True Crime, Claymore Press, Frontline Books, Praetorian Press, Seaforth Publishing and White Owl

For a complete list of Pen & Sword titles please contact:

PEN & SWORD BOOKS LTD
47 Church Street, Barnsley, South Yorkshire, S70 2AS, UK.
E-mail: enquiries@pen-and-sword.co.uk
Website: www.pen-and-sword.co.uk

or

PEN AND SWORD BOOKS,
1950 Lawrence Road, Havertown, PA 19083, USA
E-mail: Uspen-and-sword@casematepublishers.com
Website: www.penandswordbooks.com

MIX
Paper | Supporting responsible forestry
FSC® C013604
FSC www.fsc.org

Contents

Introduction

The United Kingdom has, for many hundreds of years, produced a long line of wartime heroes and leaders with the names of Lord Nelson and the Duke of Wellington heading the list of such people.

While Horatio Nelson tops this list, losing his life and saving his nation at the moment of his greatest triumph during the Battle of Trafalgar in 1805, Arthur Wellesley, the Duke of Wellington, managed a series of victories over Napoleon Bonaparte which culminated with the Battle of Waterloo in 1815 and the dismissal of the dictator once and for all.

While both men served at the front and managed to block the plans of Napoleon Bonaparte, a man many consider to have been an evil dictator, similar leaders and heroes who served on the front line are harder to find in the First and Second World Wars.

Very few senior commanders like Nelson and Wellington ventured onto the front line during the two world wars and while there were thousands of acts of gallantry, few can sadly be remembered by the general public today. Even the names of those who won the Victoria Cross are mostly forgotten in the mists of time, but one man, many people do remember, mainly due to the 1955 movie *The Dambusters*, is Wing Commander Guy Penrose Gibson.

The movie for decades was seen as a rite of passage for many people, especially teenage boys who dreamt of flying, while the portrayal of Gibson by actor Richard Todd was reputed to have been very accurate. Richard Todd, himself a former paratroop officer who dropped into France on 6 June 1944, is said to have spoken with a number of officers and airmen who had personally known Gibson in a bid to recapture his character and mannerisms. It is said he also consulted Guy Gibson's widow Eve, and the designer of the bouncing bomb Sir Barnes Wallis.

The 1955 movie, although deemed to be one of the best war films ever made, is now somewhat dated and it awaits a modern CGI assisted remake. The 'Upkeep' mine, or to use its regular moniker, the bouncing bomb, was still on the secret list in 1955 and very little technical detail was included in the film. In addition, historians have since identified a number of inaccuracies with the 1955 movie, but none of these have diminished the aurora that still surrounds the central character of Wing Commander Guy Gibson.

Guy Gibson was a distinguished pilot before the Dams raid, having served a tour of bomber operations with No. 83 Squadron and then another on night-fighters with No. 29 Squadron in Kent. When his tour on night-fighters was complete, rather than undertake a post as a flying instructor, Gibson was given command of No. 106 Squadron, converting the unit to Lancasters and making it one of the most efficient units in Bomber Command.

At the age of just twenty-four years, Guy Gibson was an acting Wing Commander with a Distinguished Service Order

(DSO), as well as the Distinguished Flying Cross (DFC) and bar. The citations to these awards described him as an energetic, efficient, skilful pilot and leader, but what was he really like?

What many movie viewers do not know, is that Guy Gibson would only survive another sixteen months after the May 1943 Dams raid, being killed on an operation to control the target marking and bombing of the German towns of Mönchengladbach and Rheydt on 19 September 1944. With less than eight months until the conclusion of the European war, his loss seems like so many others to have been completely pointless.

After the Dams raid, Guy Gibson was awarded the Victoria Cross and feted across the free world. The award of the Victoria Cross was no surprise. The citations for his DFCs and DSOs spoke of his utmost courage and devotion to duty, his flying skills, particularly at low-level, his courageous leadership, his outstanding determination and the setting of a fine example to his crews were consistently mentioned. With two tours of operations on bombers and one on night-fighters, he had flown over one hundred and seventy operations and shot down three enemy aircraft while damaging a number of others. He was, in mid-1943, arguably the finest example of an RAF pilot.

After receiving his Victoria Cross, Guy Gibson went on a tour with Prime Minister Winston Churchill to North America, where he was acclaimed as a hero, before he returned to Britain at the end of the year. He was even conferred *Commander of the Legion of Merit* by President Franklin D. Roosevelt in October 1943.

Many people have assumed Guy Gibson continued with his operational service before being killed in 1944, but the story is very different and the hero was struggling with a form of post-dams blues. He changed as a character, but what caused this and who was responsible for this?

At one point, he became the prospective parliamentary candidate for the constituency of Macclesfield in Cheshire, but nothing could cool his wish to return to action and even his marriage to Eve started to breakdown.

Like a caged tiger, Guy Gibson, who had spent most of his adult life on the front line, wanted to return to his famous No. 617 Squadron and the world he thrived in, but he was effectively banned from operations, being told not to fly over enemy territory.

Left to kick his heels, Gibson was sent on further publicity tours and a Staff Officers course, before being asked to write his autobiography, a book that would become an international best seller in 1946, titled *Enemy Coast Ahead.* By 1944, Gibson's marriage was in crisis and he found himself outside the circle of operational airmen, people he had known for most of his adult life. Desperate to be acknowledged and remembered, Guy Gibson had a number of run-ins and was possibly jealous of his successor on 617 Squadron.

Eventually, having just turned twenty-six years of age, he managed to orchestrate what would become his final operational flight, but how he died has always been the subject of controversy and speculation ever since. Guy Gibson's de Havilland Mosquito crashed in a ball of flame at Steenbergen in the Netherlands at about 10:30pm (BST) on the evening of 19 September 1944, killing its pilot and his navigator – Squadron Leader James Warwick DFC.

Whether Guy Gibson was shot down by the enemy or friendly forces is a constant subject of debate. Could it have been a technical failure on the aircraft? Was Gibson and his navigator, Squadron Leader James Warwick, adequately trained to fly this final mission? Was the aircraft serviceable or could it have been sabotaged? There is also the weather to consider, with many bombers encountering a storm over the Netherlands that night.

Over many years, there have been many air crashes caused by a combination of more than one issue, the question is whether there was more than one factor which led either directly or indirectly to Guy Gibson's death?

To try and identify how the legend Guy Gibson died that night, we must not only examine the events leading to the crash, but also the man himself, his character and his experience of life. Could events over the previous years have been partly responsible for his death? Could his upbringing have contributed that night in 1944 and what did people really think and say about his behaviour?

Guy Gibson is a British war hero and this book is not an attempt to diminish that characterisation. This is merely an attempt to examine his death and to try and explain what happened that night. Some of the facts contained within this book may diminish the eighty years old image of Guy Gibson, while others may increase the aurora surrounding this man. The fact is, none of us are perfect and Guy Gibson was just another human being. He had a traumatic upbringing and was thrust as a young man into the maelstrom of the Second World War. Like many people, he found some relationships difficult, but he had an overpowering desire to be successful and the best there could be.

As a former Senior Investigating Officer (SIO) in the police, I was trained to investigate deaths and one of the important elements of any inquiry, was knowing the character and prior behaviour of the deceased, especially leading up to their time of death. This in many instances was a contributory factor, large or small to that person's death.

Sadly, the vast majority, if not all of the witnesses contained within this book, are no longer with us in late 2024. I have therefore searched through a vast amount of material to gather the comments of those witnesses and compare the information with that contained within official records. It is also worth bearing in mind that there have been countless editions of Gibson's book *Enemy Coast Ahead,* some of the more recent versions being able to provide much of the information the censors removed from the first few editions.

I would like to thank the UK National Archives, RAF Museum at Hendon, RAF Air Historical Branch, the Imperial War Museum, the International Bomber Command Centre in association with Lincoln University and the Pathfinders archive for their assistance in writing this book. Thanks also go to the Grantham Library for their assistance in relation to the Grantham Journal archives.

The statements of individuals, held in the audio archives of the International Bomber Command Centre and the Imperial War Museum, were recorded many decades after the events they relate to. Both archives cannot guarantee and nor can I, that the verbal statements contained within each recording and transcribed in this book, are one hundred per cent accurate. I would therefore ask readers to use their own judgement in considering this evidence.

This is the story of Guy Gibson as a character and an examination of his death on the evening of 19 September 1944. All I ask is the reader be open-minded when they read this new biography of one of the greatest of the Second World War's heroes.

Chapter One

The Making of the Man

On 12 August 1918, Leonora Mary Gibson gave birth to her third child, a baby boy who would be christened Guy Penrose Gibson. Guy was born in Shimla, in the state of Himachal Pradesh, India, his father, Alexander James Gibson, being an officer in the Imperial Indian Forestry Service.

Baby Guy's middle name Penrose was a Cornish name and was given in recognition of his family's Cornish ancestry. Guy Gibson had an elder brother, Alexander Edward Charles, who was born in June 1915 and a sister, Joan, who was born in August 1916. His brother was known to the family as Alick, while Guy's father, Alexander James Gibson, was often known from his initials as A.J. while his mother was usually known as Nora rather than Leonora.

Guy spent his early years in Northern India in the family home, a relatively cozy existence with servants in a large house and manicured gardens. He was part of a comfortable upper-middle class family and very much part of the ruling elite in the jewel of the British Empire.

In 1924, at the age of just six years, Guy was sent back to England for his schooling. He was sent with his sister Joan to a boarding school in Cornwall, but they spent holidays with their grandmother in Porthleven, near Helston, rather than returning home to India, a sea journey that would take many weeks. The young Guy therefore received very little parental contact and guidance during his early formative years, most of it coming from his schoolmasters and his grandmother.

In 1926, Guy was sent to St George's Preparatory School in Earl's Avenue, Folkestone, Kent, where his brother Alick was already boarding. Little is known about his time at St. George's School, but in September 1932, aged fourteen years, Guy was sent to board at St. Edward's School in Oxford.

St. Edward's School had an excellent reputation and this would be further enhanced during the Second World War. Not only did Guy Gibson attend, but so too did Douglas Bader, the charismatic, legless fighter pilot who would similarly become a wartime hero. Others included Wing Commander Adrian Warburton DSO* DFC** and two winners of the George Cross – Pilot Officer Raymond Lewin and Sergeant Arthur Banks. The spirit of aviation pervaded throughout the school and other alumni included Geoffrey de Havilland and John Carver Meadows Frost, the aircraft designers. De Havilland, coincidentally, designing the Mosquito aircraft Gibson would be killed flying in late 1944.

The school had a thriving pre-war Officer Training Corps (OTC) which was strict and involved regular drill and leadership exercises. Guy Gibson became a Lance Corporal in the OTC. Whatever their methods, one in three boys from the establishment who joined the Royal Air Force, would be decorated for gallantry during the Second World War.

The day-to-day schooling at St. Edward's was strict, with a harsh disciplinary regime and it is said Gibson performed the role of a *fag* for an older boy, but was bullied because of his lack of height and stature.

Hand in hand with this restrict disciplinary regime was religious education and the boys prayed every day. These were the environmental conditions of St. Edward's School, which produced leaders such as Guy Gibson, Douglas Bader and others. Both Gibson and Bader would in time, be seen as being somewhat bombastic and even arrogant, but they got the job done and led from the front.

Sport was important at St. Edward's and despite his physical size, Guy Gibson played rugby and was by all accounts, a half decent cricketer. Outside of school he liked dinghy sailing, a skill he learnt while on holiday in Cornwall and which he continued until his death whenever time permitted.

Academically, Guy Gibson did not excel, but he was intelligent and had an inquisitive mind – especially when it came to technology. He liked reading, especially the Arthurian Legends and Shakespeare, his favourite play being *Henry V*.

After the Dams raid in May 1943, an official RAF photographer took a series of colour images of Gibson and his crews. One image depicts Gibson lying in a field of poppies reading a copy of Sir Thomas Malory's *Le Morte D'Arthur*. From his reading preferences, it would appear he was engrossed with battles, leadership and glory.

Although he loved the sea and dinghy sailing, Gibson, like many young men in the 1930s, was very interested in flying and an admirer of the First World War fighter ace Albert Ball. Like Gibson, Albert Ball had been a member of his own school's OTC and was religious, he was an average student and also mechanically minded. Sadly, like Gibson, Ball would be killed in action in 1917, but he only received his Victoria Cross post mortem. It is said Gibson had an image of the ace on his bedroom wall, rather like any teenager today would adorn their wall with their heroes.

At one point, Gibson wrote to the famous test pilot Joseph 'Mutt' Summers asking his advice on flying. It is said, Summers advised him to join the Royal Air Force and in 1936, Gibson applied to become a pilot. (Fate would decree that 'Mutt' Summers would meet Gibson again, as he was the test pilot on the Dambuster experimental flights a few years later in 1943.)

Unfortunately, Gibson's initial application for military pilot training was rejected, apparently because his legs were too short, but not to be put off, he applied again some months later and was successful. When he left St. Edward's School, Gibson was just 5'6" tall, but of good health and physical stature. He was described as having light brown wavy hair, blue eyes and good teeth. Despite being judged to be in good health, Gibson did occasionally suffer with migraines, something that would preclude him from pilot training in this day and age.

Guy attended No. 6 Civilian Flying Training Course at Yatesbury near Bristol at the end of 1936. The winter weather was poor and there were gaps in the flying training schedule, leading to the students having to stay inside and study. Eventually, Gibson passed, but his ground school results were not particularly impressive and his flying was only passed as average.

Having left Yatesbury, Gibson attended No. 24 (Training Group) RAF Uxbridge for basic officer training. In early

1937, he passed out as an Acting Pilot Officer on a short-term commission and was sent to No. 6 Flying Training School at Netheravon in Wiltshire, for more advanced pilot training.

In May 1937, less than a year after joining the RAF, he was awarded his pilots wings. Officially, he was an average pilot with somewhat average academic ground school results, but in six years he would rise to become a Wing Commander with the Victoria Cross, Distinguished Service Order and bar and Distinguished Flying Cross and bar; plus, three aerial victories as a night-fighter pilot. He was certainly a fine example of a late developer.

On 4 September 1937, Guy Gibson was posted to No. 83 Squadron at RAF Turnhouse near Edinburgh. The unit flew the Hawker Hind, but a year later they exchanged them for the larger Handley-Page Hampden bomber. Although his service record showed him to be an average, steady pilot and not a risk taker, he soon developed a love of low-flying, something that would follow his career to his death on 19 September 1944.

In 1938, after converting to Hampden's, No. 83 Squadron moved south to RAF Scampton near Lincoln – a station forever to be associated with Gibson and the Dambusters.

Guy Gibson was allegedly not a favourite among his fellow officers, some thinking him a little arrogant and too keen on discussing his own flying abilities with an enhanced ego. In addition, his upper-middle class boarding school background, appears to have engendered an inability to communicate with non-commissioned officers and the lower ranks. This particular trait was one that would be mentioned repeatedly over the next eighty years by witnesses. In fact, the young officer was known to No. 83 Squadrons' groundcrews as the 'Bumptious Bastard' among other things. Many minor technical faults on his aircraft would prompt a petulant outburst from the young nineteen year old Pilot Officer, much to the annoyance of the poor suffering groundcrews.

It is said the actor Richard Todd spent many months perfecting his portrayal of Gibson for the Dambusters movie, speaking with Gibson's widow and many of those who knew him; but clearly, he chose to ignore any comments about his petulant behaviour – assuming he ever heard any of these accounts.

In the movie, there is a scene where Gibson briefs his aircrews which is particularly memorable. He stands on the briefing room stage, bolt upright, hands on his hips with his chest puffed out. In another scene, he emphasises a point by telling them to get it right, raising his voice at the end of his sentence with the word 'right'; while in another Gibson tells the men to keep their mouths shut for reasons of secrecy, again with particular emphasis on the word 'shut'. This we are told was a fine portrayal of Guy Gibson and together with the less than sympathetic comments about his personality, we can get a pretty good vision of the man. He was forthright, to the point of being rude and some would think over bearing – perhaps a case of what we know as *little man syndrome*?

The young Gibson, before he was a squadron commander, continued his low-flying and did take some risks, even if they were calculated ones, with No. 83 Squadron. In October 1938, he was charged with negligence following an incident in which he taxied his Hawker Hind into a large mower at RAF Hemswell in Lincolnshire. The subsequent Court of Inquiry found him guilty and he was fined, but this would not be the last time the young officer showed a lack of judgement and ended up being fined.

In early 1939, Gibson's short-term commission was due to expire, but such was the state of European affairs and the probable impending war, he was retained. He remained with No. 83 Squadron, but the 'Bumptious Bastard' was still causing problems for lesser mortals. On page 34 of his book *Guy Gibson,* Richard Morris recounts how the young officer would sit in the cockpit of his Hampden with the switches knowingly turned-off, while the poor groundcrews cranked the engines over and over again without an ignition. Why he would do this to the men who serviced and cared for his aircraft is unknown, but he certainly was on this evidence, an uncaring 'Bumptious Bastard'.

In August 1939, Gibson turned twenty-one. The following month, war was declared on 3 September and Gibson flew with six Hampdens to attack the German Naval fleet off the port of Wilhelmshaven in the Baltic Sea.

In his later autobiography *Enemy Coast Ahead,* Gibson said he was very nervous and regularly had to use the toilet before take-off. The weather turned out to be atrocious and they returned without even sighting the enemy ships.

Shortly afterwards, his brother and sister presented him with his twenty-first birthday present – a gold watch. However, according to Susan Ottaway in her book *Dambuster,* Gibson shocked his siblings by thanking them both, but asked why they had bought him it. He explained prophetically, that in his own opinion, he was already a dead man and did not expect to survive the coming war.

Although he flew his first operation on 3 September 1939, it would be many weeks and months before his next, this was due in part to the atrocious winter weather and the so-called 'Phoney War', but also other unforeseen circumstances. In September, Guy was bitten by another officer's dog as he patted it on the head. Although he loved dogs, he received a deep wound that would require a number of stitches and had his arm placed in a sling, keeping him off operations.

The issue of female company is something that has always been an oddity with Guy Gibson. Although he casually mentions girls in his own book *Enemy Coast Ahead,* they are not named and neither are any other details. As we shall see throughout this book, he did fraternize with women, even after he was married, but he was also chivalrous and did not name names.

In December 1939, Gibson went on leave and visited his brother Alick in the Midlands. One night he went into Coventry and attended a review called, *Come out to play* at the New Hippodrome. In the chorus line that night, was a good looking twenty-eight year old woman named Evelyn Moore, who was usually called Eve by her friends. Guy, who was apparently sat in the front row, was struck by her long legs and pretty face. He was by all accounts totally smitten.

Gibson always said they met at an after show party, but in later years, Eve would say he was sat in the front row of the stalls and was there again over the following two nights – in fact at the time, it caused her some concern. In modern parlance he was acting like a stalker. On the fourth night in a row, he sent a message to her dressing room asking if they could meet after the show. Despite her apparent concerns, she agreed to meet the 21-year-old pilot.

Guy would become infatuated by her and Eve later recalled he drank a lot of alcohol and eventually asked if she had a boyfriend. When she told him she was single, he asked somewhat immaturely, if he could become her boyfriend and she agreed.

The couple met again the following night and addresses were exchanged. Eve, in later years, would recall that despite having quite a lot of alcohol, Guy drove off in *an erratic manner* in his old Rover car. Just like his charge for negligence in October 1938, the 21-year-old junior officer was still showing a lack of judgement and recklessness, something we do not associate with the man retrospectively. The next day, Guy returned to his squadron at Scampton.

The winter of 1939-40 was quite cold and there was little opportunity for flying, especially operationally with No. 83 Squadron.

Guys parents were now back in England, but they had separated. Apart from his contact with his brother and sister, Guy had little contact with his mother Nora. She had started drinking heavily and had been admitted to a clinic to try and abate her dependency. He also saw very little of his father. In many ways service life and now Eve were the centre of Gibson's universe, everything centred around them.

Prior to Christmas 1939, Nora Gibson left her clinic and went to live in Kensington, London. Living in a small bedsit like room, just before Christmas, her clothing caught fire on an unguarded electrical heater (some accounts say it was a stove) and she sustained severe burns to her lower body and legs. In severe pain, she was admitted to hospital, telling doctors her dress had touched the implement and caught fire. Nora survived in excruciating pain for a few days and died on the morning of Christmas Eve 1939.

How and when Guy was informed of his mother's death or the incident is something of a mystery. In his autobiography *Enemy Coast Ahead,* Gibson only mentions that there were Christmas celebrations at Scampton with the time-honoured tradition of the officers serving dinner to the airmen, but there is no mention of his own personal loss. This is not surprising as when he wrote the book in 1944, its aim was to bring his operations to the publics' attention, not to discuss his own personal life. There is also nothing noted about leave in the No. 83 Squadron Operations Record Book or its summary, although Gibson was not flying at all that month and probably still unfit for duty due to the dog bite.

In February 1940, Gibson flew two operational sweeps over the North Sea from Lossiemouth in the north of Scotland. Both were uneventful and the so-called 'Phoney War' seemed to be continuing.

Guy and Eve stayed in contact with one another and in March 1940 he surprised both Eve and her parents when he suddenly arrived on the doorstep of their home in Archer Road, Penarth, South Wales. Whether Eve had told her parents about Guy is unclear, but he arrived and Eve ended up introducing him to her shocked parents before he stayed for dinner with the family. After their dinner, Guy and Eve went out for the evening in Cardiff.

Once back with No. 83 Squadron, the weather started to improve and Guy flew a number of mine laying and reconnaissance operations over the North Sea and the Kattegat area off Denmark. These apparently uneventful missions continued into May 1940, before he had his first close shave with death on 17 May.

The target that night was Hamburg and Gibson and his crew dived their Hampden through the flak to drop their bombs, but in the process, they managed to snare a barrage balloon cable on the starboard wing. The thick cable damaged the slat on the edge of the wing, before winding itself around the base of the starboard propellor. Somehow, Gibson managed to fly his disabled Hampden home, landing at Abingdon in Oxfordshire due to thick fog at RAF Scampton.

Over the next month, during the Battle of France, Gibson flew a number of operations against canals, airfields and railway lines. On 29 June, his Hampden was hit and damaged by anti-aircraft fire, but he still managed to return home unscathed. As the month of June 1940 concluded, he had completed twenty-three operational sorties.

The following month, No. 83 Squadron were briefed to attack the feared German battleship *Scharnhorst* at Kiel on 1 and 4 July and Guy Gibson took part in both operations. On the first he made what he believed was a successful dive-bombing attack upon the ship, but he did not see his bombs explode and could not say whether he hit the vessel. On 4 July, Gibson returned to the same target with his squadron, but this time he reportedly made five practice dives before he finally released his bombs, which overshot the target and struck some of the buildings in the town of Kiel.

These assaults upon the heavily defended shipyards, took the crews of No. 83 Squadron by surprise, but it was clear Gibson was determined to hit his target and get his attack right, even in the face of such a heavy defensive barrage.

Guy Gibson's tenacity, bravery and determination were beginning to get him noticed, not just among his squadron colleagues, but at higher command and on 8 July, he was awarded the Distinguished Flying Cross (DFC), having completed twenty-five operational flights and being just twenty-one years of age.

Gibson could be very outspoken and air force legend states that as a young Flying Officer in the summer of 1940, he was first noticed by the later Commander-in-Chief of Bomber Command – Arthur Harris. It is said that during one of his visits to Scampton, as No. 5 Group AOC to review No. 83 Squadron, the young Flying Officer confronted Harris about the lack of rearward defensive armament on the Hampden. Gibson must have made quite an impression on his AOC as the single gun was soon replaced with a stronger armament. The short, 21-year-old pilot, who had a DFC on his chest, had the temerity to challenge the Air Officer Commanding, but he had certainly been noticed.

On 9 July, the squadron attacked the battleship *Tirpitz,* which was nearing completion in the shipyards of Wilhelmshaven. Gibson pressed home his attack in the face of heavy anti-aircraft fire and barrage balloons, but once again, he did not see the result of his bombs.

A few days later, Gibson was part of a formation that attacked a target near Dortmund, but on 27 August 1940, he showed his low-flying skills by dropping a number of sea mines, before attacking an E-Boat and a searchlight with his machine guns. His flying logbook claimed the E-Boat to be damaged and the searchlight to be extinguished.

The following night, the 28 August, Gibson and his crew attacked a target near Lorient, but were unsuccessful, having to bring their bombs home. They did however, according to Gibson's logbook entry, encounter a Dornier 17 which his gunners engaged, claiming it as probably destroyed. However, the No. 83 Squadron Operations Record Book does not mention the encounter with the Dornier.

Another close shave with death occurred on 20 September 1940, during an attack on Antwerp. An anti-aircraft shell passed through the bottom of the cockpit hitting the rudder bar and narrowly missing Gibsons feet. The force of the shell sent the rudder bar swinging into the unfortunate bomb aimer – Sergeant Houghton – who was sat just below Gibson in the aircrafts nose. Houghton was knocked senseless and the internal intercom was also knocked out. Gibson managed to fly the damaged Hampden home, where he was the butt of some hilarity, with some of his colleagues claiming his short legs had saved his feet and even his life!

Three days later, Gibson flew his last operational flight with No. 83 Squadron in an attack on Potsdamer Station. Upon his successful return, he had completed a total of thirty-nine operational flights.

Guy Gibson was now recognised by his senior officers, both locally and at Group and Bomber Command, as an officer who would always press on in the face of heavy defensive fire. He also seemed to be a natural leader of men. At a time when his squadron had lost nineteen aircraft and over fifty of his colleagues, including three Squadron Leaders and three Flight Lieutenants, Gibson was an apparent survivor, but he desperately needed a rest. He was therefore posted to No. 14 Operational Training Unit (OTU) at RAF Cottesmore in Rutland to train new bomber crews. Like many of his tour expired colleagues, he did not fancy the job of training newbies. This could often be more dangerous than operations, so he immediately tried to return to front line duties.

Gibson was granted a period of leave before he took up the position at the Cottesmore OTU and he joined Eve at her parents' home in Penarth for a short holiday. Eve however, was in for a shock, as Guy now planned on marrying her.

Guy's own family had almost disintegrated. His mother was dead and he hardly saw his brother and sister, while his father, who was back in England, was making a new life for himself with another woman.

Gibson who appeared at times to be a brash and confident young officer, was actually a man who needed a family and stability. Whether a woman almost seven years his senior could satisfy this need was debatable. What was not debatable, was the fact he loved Eve and was infatuated with her.

Gibson was in a hurry, he still believed he could die in action at any time. After all, he had seen so many of his colleagues killed or posted missing. He was not a romantic and the proposal when he made it, was not one made on a chivalrous bended knee. On their way to the Moore family home in Penarth, Guy asked Eve to marry him. Eve recalled accepting the proposal straight away, he was after all, a young handsome pilot with a DFC and she was approaching thirty years of age. Their engagement was announced by Eve's family in the local newspaper and a date set in December 1940 for the wedding.

Whether Guy had told Eve he was trying to return to the front line is unclear, but almost immediately, Guy was posted once again, this time to RAF Upper Heyford and No. 16 Operational Training Unit. His time at Cottesmore, which included his leave and the marriage proposal was just two weeks.

RAF Upper Heyford was no improvement on Cottesmore, No. 16 OTU trained bomber crews on Hampdens and it was not to Guy's liking, but a rescuer was about to pluck him from this malaise.

At the end of the Battle of Britain, the Luftwaffe turned its attention to night-time bombing and the blitzing of British cities. The RAF had few night-fighter pilots and even fewer aircraft capable of dealing with the blitz. RAF Fighter Command was not only short of night-fighter aircraft, but experienced and competent crews with nocturnal experience. To counter this deficiency, Air Vice-Marshal Trafford Leigh-Mallory, supported by his long-time supporter Air Marshal Sholto Douglas, approached Bomber Command to loan some experienced bomber pilots. The hope was not only would they perform well, but they would pass on their knowledge of night flying and experience to the younger inexperienced night-fighter crews.

Air Marshal Arthur Harris, Deputy Chief of the Air Staff at the time, agreed with this proposal and sent a number of pilots to assist Fighter Command. One such pilot was Guy Gibson, a pilot he became aware of while previously in command of No. 5 Group, to which No. 83 Squadron belonged. Why Harris decided to send one of his most promising young bomber pilots is unclear, perhaps he thought he would be safer flying night-fighters, rather than training new bomber crews, but he probably hoped to have Guy Gibson return in time, as a new squadron commander. Harris, it was claimed, told Gibson he could return to an operational squadron once he had completed his time on night-fighters.

Flight Lieutenant Guy Gibson was sent to No. 29 Squadron at RAF Digby in Lincolnshire, arriving on 13 November 1940. In his own autobiography, *Enemy Coast Ahead,* Gibson makes no mention of the request from Fighter Command or any conversation he had with Air Marshal Arthur Harris. Instead, he tells the story of the *Battle of the Snake-pit,* an on-going grudge between fighter and bomber command pilots in Lincolnshire. Gibson added that his role in the battle, 'Had been brief, merely to be slightly rude to fighter types on occasions.' He ended the account with the sentence, 'Despite this, my hand wasn't quite as steady as it might have been, when one day in October, I received a blunt telegram from the Air Ministry:

> 'Report to 29 (F) Squadron Digby for Flight Commander (Flying) Duties. FORTHWITH.'

Chapter Two

A Change of Focus

The arrival of Flight Lieutenant Guy Gibson at No. 29 Squadron was not a warm one, something he would unfortunately encounter more than once during his illustrious career.

In October 1940, No. 29 Squadron was equipped with the Bristol Blenheim, a twin-engine multi-role aircraft, which was used as both a bomber and a day fighter, neither of which it performed with any great degree of success. The squadron was however about to convert to the much more capable radar equipped Bristol Beaufighter.

When Gibson arrived at RAF Digby and its satellite airfield at Wellingore, the unit was in a period of transformation. The squadron had started to receive the Bristol Beaufighter, an aircraft developed for night fighting with a very heavy armament of four 20mm cannons and .303 machine guns, as well as a new top secret airborne interception radar.

The squadron was not only changing its aircraft, but also its personnel and when Gibson entered the Officers' Mess at Wellingore Grange, he immediately detected a sense of open hostility. A few officers sat around lounging in arm chairs reading and while some ignored his arrival, he did at least receive the odd glance from others.

In *Enemy Coast Ahead*, Gibson recalls being introduced to the officers by the adjutant Sam France: 'Er, this is Flight Lieutenant Gibson, the new 'A' Flight commander.' But there was just silence. Gibson added, 'One or two put their newspapers down, someone even yawned, but it was obvious they weren't pleased to see me.'

To make matters worse, one officer – Peter Kells – got up, walked out and slammed the door on the way out. It was not a happy place. Despite this atmosphere, there were some friendly officers and Gibson soon struck up a friendship with Graham Little and a number of others.

The Commanding Officer of No. 29 Squadron was 31-year-old Wing Commander Charles Widdows, an experienced pilot and a new commanding officer. Gibson soon discovered that although he first found him, 'A little pompous,' he soon grew to like his new Commanding Officer.

Charles Widdows was an experienced former test pilot who had been given command of the squadron in June 1940. He found it to be an inefficient unit and he quickly identified a degree of slackness and associated low morale amongst the air crews. Widdows set about rooting out the poorly performing pilots and radar operators, replacing them with young men like Guy Gibson. This was the reason for the atmosphere when bomber pilot Guy Gibson entered the Officers' Mess.

Guy Gibson respected Charles Widdows and in many ways, his later command of Nos. 106 and 617 Squadrons would reflect the attitude of his new commanding officer. Widdows was always fair, but he was intolerant of indiscipline and untidiness, while he did not approve of any familiarity between officers and other ranks, even in the air. Off duty in the Officers' Mess, Widdows was relaxed and sociable just like Guy Gibson, but in the air, he was an ace pilot, winning the respect of his men. This would be the template for Gibson's later commands.

It was clear Guy Gibson would have to make his mark on No. 29 Squadron and lead by example, something he was always keen to do. The adjutant, Sam France, told Gibson that another popular officer had been expected to take command of 'A' Flight and when he arrived, the officer had to revert to his old rank and position. It was not well received by members of the flight and to make matters worse, Gibson was a decorated bomber pilot and No. 29 Squadron had been at the centre of the *Battle of the Snake-pit*; an episode by his own admission, Gibson had encountered with No. 83 Squadron.

After a few weeks of settling into life at Digby and Wellingore, Gibson took some leave and went to Penarth to marry Eve. In a fairly blasé manner, Gibson states in *Enemy Coast Ahead* that, 'On 22 November, there is an entry in my logbook which indicates that a Blenheim, flown by myself, took off to land at Cardiff aerodrome with P/O Lovell as passenger, and in the duty column, are three great words: "To be married!"'

Gibson then added, 'The only other comment I should like to make, is that this was due to the courtesy of Cox and King's Bank, London, who granted me an overdraft of £5 for the occasion.'

Although *Enemy Coast Ahead* was written in 1944 and as we shall see, his relationship with Eve was diminishing, the comment about an overdraft of £5 to marry the love of his life seems a strange comment to make. Surely, he could have added that he was so happy and proud at the time to be marrying Eve? In many respects the comment about the money places the spotlight on himself and not his new bride, was he trying to say how much he was doing or giving up for her? Was this an arrogant comment and reflective of his own egotistical personality?

The wedding was a small affair, Eve wearing a traditional white dress and her parents and brother attending. From Guy's side there were few relatives, his siblings attended as well as his father who had a new young wife accompanying him. She was introduced to Guy, but no comment was made or recorded about his new stepmother.

After the wedding ceremony and a small reception, the newly-weds took a short honeymoon in a small hotel near the River Severn, but Guy was already itching to return to his unit and action. Within a few days, the couple arrived in Lincolnshire and found a small room at The Lion pub in Wellingore. What Eve must have thought of her new home can only be imagined. She would be left alone in a small room all night, while her new husband went off on his nightly patrols.

Guy and most of his squadron had now converted to the Bristol Beaufighter and was making night-time patrols off the coast of Lincolnshire and Norfolk. Initially, he did not have a regular or dedicated radar operator and on 10 December, he chased what turned out to be a friendly aircraft. The following night, he chased and lost a Junkers 88 over the North Sea, firing off an apparently ineffective long-range burst as the fleeing bomber disappeared from sight.

On 20 December, Gibson spotted another enemy aircraft, but lost it and could not open fire. The following morning at 08:15hrs, Gibson was airborne when he witnessed a Junkers 88 shot down by the anti-aircraft guns near Manby in Lincolnshire. Throughout the dark winter nights, Gibson and his varying radar operators patrolled the skies, but they were unable to bring any bombers down.

Gibson, a man who was desperate for action and success was frustrated. At least as a bomber pilot he could drop bombs on a stationary target, but as a night-fighter he had to find the constantly moving enemy and the airborne radar was not always effective.

In February 1941, Gibson linked up with Sergeant Richard 'Jimmy' James, a man who would become his regular radar operator while with No. 29 Squadron. While the two built a good professional relationship in the air, Gibson's own pre-war officer mentality prevented the two men from becoming less formal in the air. Gibson would call James by his rank or his surname, while he expected his radar operator to call him sir.

Gibson appears to have been very aware of his own mortality as we saw when he was given the gold watch by his siblings just after the war had started. In *Enemy Coast Ahead,* he describes never being very squeamish about bodies, but one night a Wellington bomber crashed on the airfield and he described going out to the wreckage the next morning.

The RAF bomber which was burned out was now a charred skeleton, Gibson describing, 'We could see quite clearly the pilot sitting at his controls burnt to a frazzle, with his goggles gently swaying in the wind, hanging from his hand.' This ghoulish detail in a wartime autobiography, by a wartime pilot who had already indicated the likelihood of his own death, is one that could keep the psychologists busy for quite some time. What seems even stranger is the fact Gibson and fellow night-fighter John 'Bob' Braham would both appropriate life jackets from shot-down Luftwaffe aircrew and wear them on operations, deeming them to be a better quality than their own British versions. (Gibson would wear this life jacket on the Dams raid and was possibly wearing it when he died in September 1944.)

As the No. 29 Squadron crews started to gain in experience with the Beaufighter and its airborne radar, they started to destroy enemy bombers in early 1941.

On the night of 14–15 March, Gibson and James found a Heinkel III off Skegness. Gibson settled in behind and just below the bomber ready to open fire, but when he pressed the gun button they failed to operate. He tried again, but just one cannon fired. The Heinkel carried on and Gibson thought his gun fire must have killed the rear gunner, as there was no return fire. James had by this time vacated his radar set and was trying to remove the blockage in the cannons. He eventually managed to unblock the guns and Gibson moved back into a firing position and shot the bomber down off Skegness, the aircraft landing in the sea near the town's pier.

The aircraft which was flown by swimmer and 1936 Olympic silver medallist, Leutnant Georg Stugg of 2/KG1, and was en route to bomb Glasgow. Stugg and his crew of three were killed.

Gibson recalled the combat and its aftermath in *Enemy Coast Ahead:* After dawn, Gibson went with the squadron adjutant Sam France to Skegness, where they collected part of the Heinkel's tail as a trophy. The local Chief Constable told them there was a Hauptmann with an Iron Cross in the mortuary with his head nearly blown off by a cannon shell. Gibson said he was nearly sick, but he wanted the Iron Cross to send home to the officer's family. When he asked for the medal the police officer told him it had now been stolen, along with the man's watch. Gibson called the thieves vultures, but that did not stop him taking a rubber dinghy which he would use in Cornwall while on leave – not to forget his later appropriated German life jacket.

While Guy Gibson appears to have worked to the airmen's chivalrous code of ethics in wanting to send personal items back to a fallen man's family, he was only too happy to take parts of the aircraft, life jackets and a dinghy for himself.

This account in *Enemy Coast Ahead* does not quite correspond with the known facts about the crew of the Heinkel. Georg Stugg was a Leutnant, not a Hauptmann and his crew were all Unteroffiziers. However, Stugg, who had flown during the Battle of Britain as well as the night blitz, was the holder of the Iron Cross 1st and 2nd class. Was Gibson making a small error or had he or an unknown *ghost writer* raised Stugg's rank to enhance the victory and the story?

Gibson was now a married man and a flight commander and it appears taking life much more seriously. However, he got into the habit of removing the blackout masks from the headlights of his own car. One night the police stopped him and he ended up in the local Magistrates Court. His defence in his own words in *Enemy Coast Ahead* was simple: the visibility was down to 400 yards which is termed fog and in order to drive safely, he removed the covers. Gibson even brought the station meteorological officer to court to back up his account, but it was to no avail and he was fined four pounds and five shillings. For the second time in his life, he had ended up before an Inquiry or Magistrates Court. It was not the finest example a future disciplinarian squadron commander could set.

On 8 April 1941, Guy Gibson would have his latest close shave with the grim reaper.

The Luftwaffe had started to operate intruder night-fighters over Britain, with a specialized Gruppe undertaking these operations. On the night of 8 April 1941, Junkers 88C night-fighters from NJG2 based at Gilze-Rijen in Holland were stalking the airfields of eastern England.

Gibson and his radar operator, Sergeant Bell, were coming in to land at Wellingore just before midnight when they were raked by cannon and machine-gun fire. (Sergeant Richard James was away on leave at the time.)

A Junkers 88C of 3/NJG2, flown by Feldwebel Hans Hahn, had followed them into the circuit as they prepared to land. As Gibson lowered his flaps and undercarriage, the burst of fire riddled the Beaufighter, causing it to crash into the boundary hedge. Sergeant Bell was slightly injured, but once again, Guy Gibson had survived without a scratch.

It was a very lucky escape for Guy Gibson, Hans Hahn would soon be commissioned and awarded the Knights Cross, the first such honour for a German night-fighter pilot. By 12 October 1941, Hans Hahn had claimed twelve British machines before colliding with his final victim, an Airspeed Oxford near

Grantham. Both aircraft and their crews crashed to their deaths. Guy Gibson had been lucky to escape with his life, while so many other men had not.

On the night of 23 April, Gibson and the returning Sergeant James claimed an enemy aircraft damaged and two days later, No. 29 Squadron moved to No. 11 Group and West Malling, near Maidstone in Kent. Wing Commander Widdows had been pushing Fighter Command to move his new highly motivated unit into the south-east near the capital city, which had been heavily blitzed. Finally, he got his wish.

The move to West Malling was one which would have a profound effect upon Guy Gibson in more ways than one. In *Enemy Coast Ahead*, Chapter 12, Gibson immediately states:

> 'Of all the airfields in Great Britain, here, many say (including myself) we have the most pleasant… its location in the middle of hop country makes it extremely attractive to Air Force fellows. For in this country are many pubs, and good ones at that, and the inmates are fine types who have toiled and cherished the land for many centuries.'

Guy Gibson the party animal was to the fore once again at West Malling and the popular *Startled Saint, The Swan,* the *Five-Pointed Star* and the *Wheatsheaf,* to name but a few of the local pubs, were popular with the pilots and radar operators of No. 29 Squadron. (These pubs are still popular venues in 2024.) The airfield surrounded by hop farms and orchards was a very pleasant distraction from the war, while the Officers' Mess in early 1941, was the Hermitage – a large house in the nearby village.

Eve moved south with Guy and they managed to find a place in nearby East Malling. There was a large house called Clare House and it had a small annex which they rented. The annex had no bathroom facilities, but the house owners were only too happy to allow the young officer and his wife to use those in the main building. The house still stands to this day, as does the annex, but how many people today know of its association with Guy Gibson?

Life was very pleasant at West Malling and Eve engaged with the local amateur dramatics, using her stage skills in local presentations. It seems the couple were very happy and even obtained a small black labrador puppy, allegedly from a local farm. The dog, who due to his black coat was given a very non-politically correct name in 1941, would enjoy the odd beer himself and become just as famous as his owner. However, there is another account of how Guy Gibson obtained his famous black labrador and became entwined with a scout troop at Tovil in Maidstone.

The managing director of a local paper mill (Reed Paper Company, Aylesford), Colonel Sheldon, and a manager called Glad Bincham, were only too keen to assist the brave officers from West Malling with entertainment when off-duty. To entertain the officers, they would arrange parties at Ebbor House (now East Farleigh House) in Lower Road, East Farleigh, about two miles from the airfield. The parties would take place every Monday evening (readiness permitting) during the summer of 1941 and there would be a number of female guests as well.

Glad Bincham would later invite Gibson to attend his Tovil scout troop and it is said he introduced him to the small black labrador puppy. The dog was said to have belonged to Bincham's niece, but she did not have the room to keep him, therefore he was passed on to Guy Gibson.

Gibson, who was a recently married man, appears to have attended some of these parties without Eve. One female party guest was thirty-two years old Lillian Arnold, who got to know Gibson very well. Lillian, who was nine years Gibson's senior in 1941, thought he was tremendous fun and the centre of any party. According to an article in the *Aeroplane Monthly* magazine in September 1992, 'She would never meet anyone quite like him again.' The relationship was reportedly a platonic one, but as we shall see later, it is clear there was a magnetism between the young pilot and women – especially older ladies.

Despite the happy home and social life, Guy Gibson was still keen to enhance his own flying career and therefore his professional standing. He commanded 'A' Flight, but he wanted more success. Although Gibson and James would make two more victory claims between May and December 1941, the squadron collectively, had made just thirteen destroyed and probably destroyed claims, with another five enemy aircraft damaged. These totals in 1941 were more than respectable and 'B' Flight Commander John 'Bob' Braham claimed five destroyed and one probable.

The two flight commanders (Gibson and Braham) accounted for most of the claims and just five other pilots made up the full number of victories. The ambitious and competitive Guy Gibson was however, beginning to get fed up, especially with the lack of opportunities and the various technical failures. On a number of occasions, either the airborne radar went unserviceable, or his cannons failed to fire.

In his book *Night-Fighter Ace*, Tony Spooner states that although some say Guy Gibson and Bob Braham were never friends, their wives were and Joan Braham asked the couple to be godparents for their son Michael. However, in his own autobiography *Night-Fighter*, Bob Braham makes no mention of this event.

Guy Gibson as a character at West Malling can be judged by further comments in Tony Spooners book. It was said he spent little time with the ground crews and would often drive his car up to his Beaufighter before taking off. On return he would get into the car and immediately drive off. Clearly, Guy Gibson had stopped his adolescent baiting of the groundcrews, but he still avoided familiarity with them. Although Gibson liked Mess parties, having Eve living nearby and his labrador pup, he would often go home instead of to the pub or the Officers' Mess.

As already mentioned, Gibson would always call his radar operator by his rank or surname. He never used his first name or his regular nick name. 'Sticks' Gregory, John Braham's regular radar operator, told Tony Spooner that Gibson was only popular with a few people on the unit, but as a pilot he had the most guts and courage of anybody he ever knew! Again, just like on No. 83 Squadron, it appears Gibson was a bit of a 'marmite' character and you either liked him or you avoided him.

As the war progressed and he aged, the character of Gibson appeared to be changing ever so slightly. Gibson continued to display his pre-war officer and public-school attitudes, this being displayed in his relationship with non-commissioned and lower ranks. However, he was now a married man and had responsibilities as a flight commander.

Michael Allen joined No. 29 Squadron in September 1941. In his autobiography *Pursuit Through Darkened Skies*, he recalls arriving at West Malling with Harry White. The men met Guy Gibson in the Startled Saint pub on the road between the airfield and the village. Gibson was in the bar with Eve and some other officers. Gibson bought them both a beer and welcomed them, introducing them to Eve and the others.

Despite the cordiality, Gibson's character showed its other side when the two new men wrote off a Beaufighter shortly after their arrival. Gibson was not impressed and he let them know it.

Things got worse for Allen and White. One night they were airborne and left their radio channel open, blocking all communications with other aircraft and the fighter controller. To make matters worse, they were even overheard (probably by the German listening service too) discussing the identification colours of the day. When they landed, Gibson was sick of the pair and they were transferred to a Havoc unit. Gibson, like his unofficial mentor Charles Widdows, wanted his team to be the best and he did not suffer fools in his flight.

To return to May 1941, on the night of the third and fourth, Gibson and James dispatched another enemy aircraft off the Isle of Wight. Although they believed the aircraft to have been a Heinkel III, it was probably the Junkers 88 of 2/KG77 which returned home badly damaged with one crewman having bailed out.

Gibson was desperate for success and did not tolerate failure. This is abundantly clear in his book when he describes on 10 May that he saw four Heinkel III's, but his cannons jammed each time. In his flying logbook alongside this event, Gibson wrote a rude comment which was blanked out by his CO Charles Widdows with a chastising note.

Over the following five days Gibson noted in his autobiography that his cannon regularly failed, but they eventually discovered the cause was a solenoid in the gun firing button that was at fault; but he was very disappointed having missed so many opportunities to increase his personal score.

Although now an acting Squadron Leader and loving West Malling and the local area, Guy's ambitions were not being achieved and after a very active first eighteen months of the war, he probably, in his own eyes, was now underachieving. Despite this, he was awarded a bar to his Distinguished Flying Cross on 10 September 1941. The citation stated that Gibson had '*continued to show the utmost courage and devotion to duty*' before detailing his aerial victories.

In August 1987, Hugh Verity, another No. 29 Squadron pilot, who would go on to fame with the Special Duties squadrons dropping and picking up agents across Europe, audibly recorded his own wartime experiences for the Imperial War Museum. He recalled that Gibson was a very tough, merry person. He was boisterous and 'Very interested in proving himself. He was one of those people who attached great importance to decorations.' This claim about the importance of decorations is one that would be repeated by other witnesses.

After the German invasion of Russia in June 1941, the number of nocturnal visitors to Britain dramatically decreased and the chance of further glory for Gibson as a night-fighter pilot was diminishing. However, on the night of 6–7 July 1941, Gibson and James dispatched another Heinkel III near Sheerness on the Isle of Sheppey. The aircraft and its crew from 8/KG4 were lost without trace.

A period of calm followed until October 1941, when Gibson and James claimed two Junkers 87 dive-bombers destroyed over Dover in a surprise attack by the once vaunted Stukas. The two claims were not confirmed by the RAF.

Life was now easy paced at West Malling, Guy's black labrador was always welcome in the Officers' Mess, even when he relieved himself on the floor. Gibson even took the dog up in his Beaufighter on a number of occasions, but he still wanted more action.

By November, Gibson had been with the unit over a year and flown approximately ninety operational flights according to his flying logbook. He had three confirmed enemy aircraft destroyed, one probably destroyed and another three damaged. He was now an experienced night-fighter pilot as well as a bomber pilot, but he started to suspect another posting to an Operational Training Unit was just over the horizon. He therefore decided to consider Air Marshal Arthur Harris's promise to him when he left Bomber Command the previous year.

On 9 November, Gibson flew his Beaufighter to his old haunt at Scampton to see old friends. In *Enemy Coast Ahead,* Gibson recalls making what he modestly called a 'mediocre' landing by the old 'A' Flight dispersal. After exiting the aircraft, Gibson telephoned the Officers' Mess, but he soon discovered that many of his old associates were long gone, many of them killed in action.

At West Malling, Bob Braham was continuing with his own personal successes and in time, he would become one of the top night-fighter pilots along with John 'Cats eyes' Cunningham. It is possible this caused Guy Gibson some angst, especially as it looked like he was due another OTU posting.

In *Enemy Coast Ahead,* Gibson states, 'Each time I was on these stooge patrols, I used to get more and more fed up. Poor old James in the back would take a whole harangue of this being a waste of time etc.' In many ways this admission is no surprise when we consider the views of many people in relation to Gibson's behaviour, particularly to the lower ranks.

On 15 December 1941, Gibson flew to Grantham the No. 5 Group HQ to request Harris uphold his promise of the command of a bomber squadron. To Gibson's surprise, Harris had moved on and was not able to complete his promise.

The fact a Squadron Leader believed he could just turn up unannounced and demand a senior staff officer move him back to a Bomber Command unit, let alone as its CO, says an enormous amount about Guy Gibson as a character.

When Gibson returned to West Malling, his new commanding officer, Edward Colbeck-Welch, informed him that Fighter Command were transferring him to a night-fighter OTU. Upon hearing this news, Gibson decided to make a number of phone calls and pester any number of senior officers he knew.

Gibson states in *Enemy Coast Ahead* that during his last week at West Malling, he alternated with Bob Braham in trying to 'pull as many strings' as possible to avoid going to the Operational Training Unit. This he added was in addition to a series of large farewell parties.

These comments are interesting, firstly we have heard that Braham and Gibson were not that close, but Gibson appears to give an opposite view here. It also shows his continuing propensity for partying, even now he was a married man.

Exactly who Guy Gibson contacted is unclear, but Richard Morris, in his book *Guy Gibson,* speculates that he may have even contacted Sholto Douglas, the Commander-in-Chief of Fighter Command, who had been involved in the original arrangements. Whoever he contacted, his efforts appear to have failed and Gibson was sent in December to join No. 51 Operational Training Unit at Cranfield.

Gibson attended the OTU, but he was desperate to return to bombers and operations. Not surprisingly, he does not mention in detail any of his calls and efforts in *Enemy Coast Ahead,* but states that knowing Air Marshal Arthur Harris was now in charge of the entire command, he decided he would have to get back somehow to bombers (Harris had actually taken charge of Bomber Command on 22 February 1942).

In *Enemy Coast Ahead* Gibson immediately states:

> Two telegrams tell the story:
> To S/Ldr. G.P. Gibson RAF
> Date: March 12 1942: Time 10:15
> Report pm today for interview C-in-C Bomber Command. Ends.

The next:
Copy S/Ldr. G.P. Gibson RAF
Date: March 14 1942: Time 12:15
Post S/Ldr. Gibson (39438) DFC to 106 Squadron to command W/Cdr. Post. Ends.

In the book, Gibson adds as if he were surprised, 'It can be seen that the Air Marshal was certainly a fast mover.'

Somehow, Guy Gibson had managed to get through to the new Bomber Command supremo, who had adhered to his old promise and ordered the young pilot to attend his headquarters. Why 'Bomber' Harris, as he was to become known, should remember and fulfil a promise made to a 22-year-old Flying Officer is in some respects not clear. Was Guy Gibson that special and was Bomber Command desperately in need of such a character?

Bomber Command was still, in many peoples' eyes, underperforming and still using inferior aircraft such as the Stirling and Manchester to attack German cities. The new Avro Lancasters were coming into service and Harris wanted to launch a strategic air campaign against the industrial might of Germany; and Gibson was the type of squadron commander he needed.

Air Marshal Arthur Harris wrote to Air Vice-Marshal John Slessor, the Air Officer Commanding (AOC) No. 5 Group, on 22 March 1942. In the letter held in the RAF Museum, he wrote:

'I am sending you almost immediately, a Squadron Leader Guy Gibson. I understand that Fothergill, who

> commands one of your Lancaster squadrons, although a good organiser, is not a fire eater, and I am sure you will agree that these fine squadrons ought as far as possible, to have the absolute pick. Gibson has only been a Squadron Leader a year, but I desire to give him acting Wing Commander rank and command of a Lancaster squadron as soon as he can convert.'

Harris continued to sing the praises of the new man in his letter, recalling that Gibson would go out on additional night operations, 'Just for fun and attempt to bomb *Tirpitz* while she was building with 2,000lb bombs, with wing tip flares tied on to them, so he could redirect his aim next time.'

Harris noted that Gibson had been selected with other bomber pilots to assist Fighter Command with night-fighting, adding they were, 'A hand-picked bunch, of which Gibson was the best.'

The head of Bomber Command was quick to highlight that this was the fulfilment of a two year promise he had made to Gibson. He also somewhat over exaggerated, stating Gibson had accounted for seven enemy aircraft and raised 'his' squadron to an extraordinary pitch of enthusiasm and efficiency. Clearly it was nothing to do with Charles Widdows, the new CO Colbeck-Welch, or John Braham!

Charles Fothergill commanded No. 207 Squadron and this is clearly the unit Arthur Harris wanted his young protégé to command, but he allowed Air Vice-Marshal John Slessor to make the final decision. Slessor therefore posted Gibson to No. 106 Squadron, a unit equipped not with Lancasters, but it's forerunner, the poorly performing Avro Manchester. However, none of this mattered to Guy Gibson, who had once again escaped the clutches of an Operational Training Unit to return to the front line in April 1942.

Guy reportedly told his wife Eve that he was returning to command a bomber squadron and she was completely dismayed, even fearing the worst, but he was back where he believed he belonged – the new commanding officer of 106 Squadron.

Chapter Three

Return to the Heavies

After taking command of No. 106 Squadron, Guy Gibson was in no doubt he wanted his unit to be the best, not just in No. 5 Group, but in the whole of Bomber Command.

Gibson had seen how Charles Widdows had handled the difficult times with No. 29 Squadron, how he managed to forge one of the best night-fighter units in the service and now Guy wanted to replicate it with his own squadron.

After nearly three years of war and with two combat tours under his belt, Gibson had changed in many ways, but he still belonged to the pre-war RAF officer class and his public-school heritage. Although he had a propensity when he was a young officer to fracture the odd rule or two, he was now a disciplinarian and quick to form an opinion about someone, even if his initial assessment of that individual was ultimately incorrect.

As an officer and now as a commanding officer, Gibson demanded nothing but the best. While he was known as the 'Bumptious Bastard' by No. 83 Squadron's ground crews, he would soon become known as the 'Boy Emperor' to the airmen of No. 106 Squadron.

Upon arrival, he was quick to admonish the non-commissioned officers, when they failed to stand to attention as he entered the briefing room. In his book, *Enemy Coast Ahead,* Gibson even stated: 'I am afraid I was rather rude, but you have to be, so that they can know what you think and you can know what they think.' This initial meeting with their new commanding officer was quickly followed by the transfer of an unnamed non-commissioned officer whom Gibson thought was unworthy of his new elite unit.

Elsewhere, Gibson attended a party in the WAAF Mess and quietly listened to the grumbles and complaints of some of his officers, but the next morning, he held a parade and left them all in no doubt of what he expected from them. In many ways he was showing them that just because he listened, it did not mean the new commanding officer was a 'soft-touch'.

On 22 April 1942, Guy Gibson flew his first bomber operation since September 1940. The sortie in an Avro Manchester was a relatively simple *gardening* or mine-laying flight to the Baltic Sea, where they successfully planted four sea mines. Although the twin-engine Avro Manchester was a poor aircraft in terms of performance and reliability, Gibson seemed to cope well and he completed the flight without any issues.

Three nights later, Gibson led the squadron in an attack on Rostock on the Baltic coast, but with the inadequate performance of the Manchester, he was forced to attack from an altitude of just 3,500 feet. This was followed by nine days without operations, before he made another *gardening* operation just off the island of Sylt near the Danish border.

On the night of 1-2 May, Gibson remained in the operations room and was not on ops himself. One of the WAAFs engaged on administrative duties in the room was a young officer named

Mary, who had recently married Pilot Officer Harry Stoffer, a young Rhodesian pilot on No. 106 Squadron. In his book *Enemy Coast Ahead,* Gibson recalls her actions filling in the squadron state board in the operations room, 'I watched the pretty girl mount the ladder and fill in the spaces.' Mary Stoffer repeatedly climbed the ladder to chalk in the landing time of each aircraft, until just one space was left vacant – this was the aircraft of her new husband who was now missing.

> Eventually, Gibson recalls taking the stoic WAAF by the arm and leading her to his car. They stopped at the WAAF Officers Mess to collect some shopping she had purchased earlier the previous day, then he drove her to the marital home. Gibson dropped her off and added in his book with a mixture of empathy and machismo, 'There were nearly tears in my eyes as I drove home.'

Trying to judge the real character of Guy Gibson from the entries in *Enemy Coast Ahead* is difficult. Gibson clearly wanted to portray himself as a robust, no-nonsense leader, but one that is sensitive to the loss of a WAAF's new husband and fellow pilot.

Some commentators have noted the fact, Gibson mentioned Mary Stoffer was a pretty girl climbing a ladder. Was this relevant to the account, a typical 1940s comment or a Freudian slip from a man who had a wandering eye? This may be disingenuous to a man who was only showing his empathetic, caring human side, but we shall soon see that despite already being married, Gibson craved female contact, whether that be platonic or otherwise.

The squadron started to replace the poorly performing Manchester bombers, which often suffered engine failures, with the new four engine Avro Lancaster; and on 8 May, Gibson made his last operational sortie in a Manchester to Warnemünde, just north of Rostock. It was not a pleasant flight and he noted in his flying logbook that it was a 'Hot trip' with fierce opposition. The Manchester performed poorly once again and Gibson and his crew had to bomb from just 3,500 feet.

Guy Gibson would not fly operationally again for about two months, due to a period of hospitalisation at RAF Rauceby with a sinus condition, which required some minor corrective surgery. While on recuperative leave, it is said, he was angry to miss the first thousand bomber raid on Cologne at the end of May 1942.

Once recovered, Gibson converted, with the assistance of John 'Hoppy' Hopgood on to the Avro Lancaster. The two men would develop a close friendship and bond over the coming months, until Gibson personally witnessed the death of Hopgood on the Dams raid in May 1943.

On 29 May, No. 106 Squadron was declared fully operational with its new Avro Lancaster bombers. Although Gibson was still recovering from his medical condition and was off operations, that did not stop him from welcoming the Secretary of State for Air – Sir Archibald Sinclair – to Coningsby.

Gibson showed the minister around a new Lancaster before taking him up for a flight. The young CO was in his element and decided to show his guest how a Lancaster could fly on just two of its four engines. Gibson told his flight engineer to feather the two starboard engines and being suitably impressed by this demonstration, Sinclair headed off down the fuselage to inspect the rear gun turret. Gibson told the engineer to restart the engines, but the hapless and unidentified engineer feathered the other two engines, leaving the Lancaster without power. In a moment of expletive riddled panic, the four engines were quickly restarted and they made their way home. The incident and what Gibson said to his flight engineer is surprisingly not reported in *Enemy Coast Ahead* and Archibald Sinclair appears to have been completely oblivious.

Guy Gibson was determined to create an elite unit and he would interview all new aircrew arrivals. While some were welcomed with open arms, others appear to have received a very lukewarm reception from the 'Boy Emperor'. In one interview recorded by the International Bomber Command Centre and produced here with their kind permission, Sergeant Graham Allen recalls his arrival on No. 106 Squadron:

> 'We eventually got posted to 106, we were interviewed by Wing Commander Gibson and it was quite an interview believe me! They had us all standing to attention, he was very, very abrupt, an arrogant man really and anyway, we got through the interview and I always remember him saying, "Now you won't get any leave just yet, you've come here to fight and you either die or finish your tour and get a gong."'

Alex Kinnear was a sergeant and rear gunner on No. 106 Squadron and fell foul of Guy Gibson. In the *Grantham Journal* supplement - *Dambusters Remembered,* published in

1993, Alex recalled his crew getting ready for a night operation when there was a flash and their aircraft filled with smoke. With a full bomb load and brimming fuel tanks, they feared the worst and quickly evacuated their Lancaster. As they assessed the situation from a safe distance, a jeep pulled up containing Guy Gibson. The commanding officer got out and quickly told the crew, 'You've got four good engines, you'll bloody well go and bomb Germany.' Alex and his crew believed the bad-tempered Gibson was insinuating they were cowards. They eventually took off and bombed Germany, having discovered the cause of the smoke was a rogue navigation detonator, but it left a sour taste as far as they were concerned.

While Alex Kinnear says Gibson was a fine pilot and would never send anyone on an operation he wouldn't do himself, he was not keen on socialising with the lower ranks.

Alex recalled one night when his crew went to a pub in Boston and Gibson was already inside with some officers. He looked at Alex and his crew as they entered the bar, didn't say a word and turned away from them, totally ignoring them. Whether this was after the issue with the smoke-filled aircraft is not clear, but if it was, maybe Gibson was still showing his displeasure – clearly holding grudges once he had formed an opinion of a person.

There is no doubt at all that Gibson was a very good and brave pilot. Alex Kinnear recalls that one night the squadron sent six specially adapted Lancasters to attack the *Graf Zeppelin*, an aircraft carrier the Germans were constructing in Gdynia, Poland. (The raid took place on the night of 27-28 August 1942.) Cloud cover was 9/10ths over the target, so

Gibson made an astounding ten passes over the target before his bombs were released. He narrowly missed the target. The other five Lancasters had dropped their bombs and were on their way home by the time Gibson dropped his.

The five Lancasters arrived home an hour before Gibson and they assumed he had been shot down, but he soon arrived home and according to Alex Kinnear, chastised them for returning home too soon. He told them they should reduce their airspeed to conserve fuel over the North Sea, which was a safer environment and men were dying on convoys to bring fuel to the country.

In *Enemy Coast Ahead,* Gibson describes the raid on the *Graf Zeppelin* and the accompanying battle cruisers *Gneisenau* and *Scharnhorst* at Gdynia. The Admiralty were fearful of these ships getting out into the Atlantic and joining the battleship *Tirpitz,* therefore a new anti-ship bomb and bomb sight were devised, but it had to be dropped from less than 1,000 feet. Still his favourite pilot and commanding officer, Air Marshal Arthur Harris selected Gibson and No. 106 Squadron for the mission.

Gibson selected six crews, which included himself and John Hopgood for the raid. The target was covered by a haze making visibility very difficult according to Gibson and there was a lot of flak and searchlights. In the book, Gibson says he made twelve bombing runs before they released their own bomb – missing the *Gneisenau* by about 400 yards. None of the ships were hit, John Hopgood missing by about 50 yards, but again, Gibson did not mention the other aircraft returning faster than he did. In his book he recalled their flight lasted ten hours, 'And with no second pilot, I felt pretty well all in.' It appears Gibson, or a ghost writer, wanted to ensure that he was the centre of attention for any reader of *Enemy Coast Ahead.*

No. 106 Squadron were soon the best performing unit in No. 5 Group and putting up more aircraft per raid than most other units. Gibson appears to have been Harris's favourite – hence the selection for the Gdynia raid, but it also indicated that to the head of Bomber Command, Guy Gibson was a low-level, special apparatus commander, something that probably led to his selection to form No. 617 Squadron the following spring.

Alex Kinnear and his crew were soon to feel the wrath of Gibson once again. They were sent on a raid and their radio started to misbehave. Their wireless operator believed he had heard a recall order and so they returned home early. Unfortunately, it was a recall order for one aircraft with a glycol leak and when Gibson heard of their premature return, he again implied they were cowards.

Some people did get along very well with Gibson and two of these being Flight Lieutenant John 'Hoppy' Hopgood and Australian Pilot Officer Dave Shannon. Both men would join him on the Dambusters raid in May 1943. Dave Shannon joined the unit in early July 1942, but while most new pilots undertook at least one operational flight with an experienced pilot, he flew with Gibson as a second pilot on five operations between 8-21 July 1942.

In late June or early July 1942, Gibson remembers in *Enemy Coast Ahead,* talking to Squadron Leader Tommy Lloyd. Lloyd was RAF Coningsby's intelligence officer, he had flown during the First World War, won the Distinguished Service Order and clearly Gibson respected this man. During a discussion with another officer, Gibson recalls Lloyd suggesting pulling together a crack unit of Beaufighters or Mosquitos to fly in at low-level and mark the target factory with *coloured incendiaries*, before the main force plastered the area with 'cookies' (high explosive 4,000lb bombs).

This small segment was written by Gibson in early 1944, but around the same time Air Vice-Marshal Cochrane's No. 5 Group (of which Gibson was part in 1942-43 and later in mid-1944), started to introduce the same idea for target marking. Did this conversation actually occur and did Gibson include it in his book because of Cochrane's new method of target marking? Sadly, we cannot confirm this one way or the other, as Lloyd was killed in a Lancaster on 13 February 1944, when it flew into a hill in Sussex in cloud. (Coincidentally, Gibson's Dams raid flight engineer – Flight Sergeant John Pulford was also on board and killed in the accident.)

Although Tommy Lloyd had served at Coningsby from 1942-1944, the idea for Cochrane's low-level target marking is said to have come from Group Captain Sidney Bufton who worked at the Directorate of Bomber Operations at the Air Ministry. Whether the two men ever spoke and discussed this new concept is unknown, but it makes one wonder why Gibson included it in *Enemy Coast Ahead.* This seems odd, especially as we shall see later in this book, Wing Commander Leonard Cheshire was said to have been instrumental in proving this new tactic in early 1944.

While Guy Gibson appears to have preferred the company and conversation of officers rather than other ranks, he could also be a menace to the officers and even his own flight commanders.

On 18 July 1942, No. 106 Squadron took off for a raid on Essen in the Ruhr Valley. Somehow, the 'B' Flight commander, Squadron Leader John Wooldridge, took Gibson's preferred Lancaster. A talented music composer before the war, Wooldridge would go on to command the Mosquitos of No. 105 Squadron. He had a decent enough working relationship with Guy Gibson, but it was not perfect, the two men having very differing interests and outlooks on life.

Gibson and Wooldridge successfully completed the raid to Essen with Gibson taking a spare aircraft, but he was still angry when he returned, demanding a formal interview with the flight commander in his office. The outcome is unknown, although in *Enemy Coast Ahead,* Gibson gives a slightly different explanation.

Gibson was keen to state that Wooldridge was an excellent flight commander, but he also reported that his nick name was 'Dim', although he was anything but dim and wrote piano concertos. He described him as being, 'Very good with the boys, but I am afraid, rather unscrupulous with his Squadron Commander [i.e. Gibson himself].'

Prior to the mission to Essen, Gibson went to the flight servicing department and asked if he could take his favourite aircraft O-Orange on the raid. He was told the Lancaster was unserviceable with a blown engine, so he took B-Beer, an aircraft he described as a smelly, dirty, oily machine which smelt of disinfectant from the Elsan toilet in the rear fuselage.

The operation was a daylight mission and on their way home, Gibson and his crew spotted another Lancaster. They decided to formate on the Lancaster for mutual protection, but as they closed-in, they were to find it was the reportedly unserviceable O-Orange with John Wooldridge and his large handle-bar mustache at the controls. Upon realising the accompanying Lancaster was piloted by Guy Gibson, Wooldridge dived away into a layer of cloud.

In *Enemy Coast Ahead*, Gibson did not say anything about demanding a formal meeting when they landed, but he added that Dim would also carefully engineer mysterious new faces, who were transferred into his flight without Guy Gibson's knowledge.

Away from service life, the marriage of Guy and Eve was becoming much more strained. She moved to a property in St. Johns Wood, London and got a job in a factory which made camouflage netting, among other things. Guy would call her by telephone, he still loved her, but it was now a long-distance relationship. When he did visit Eve in London, he did not want to go out to the theatre or go out socialising, he just wanted to talk and rest. To make matters worse, he now wanted children and she did not. This appears to have caused a major disagreement between the couple.

At the end of September 1942, No. 106 Squadron's home base at Coningsby, which was a grass airfield, needed concrete runways laying, therefore the squadron moved to RAF Syerston in Nottinghamshire while this work was completed. Sergeant Alex Kinnear recalled that the pilots 'beat up' Coningsby with some very low flying as they left, but Gibson, a man who loved low-flying himself, was not amused. As each pilot landed his Lancaster at Syerston, he was placed under arrest pending a charge. What the outcome was is unknown, but it shows how Gibson could react in different ways.

On 17 October 1942, Gibson would get another chance to showcase his low-level flying ability.

The transformer station at Le Creusot and the power station at Montchanin in France, needed to be destroyed as they were integral to the local industry which was supporting the German war effort.

No. 5 Group's Nos. 106, 49 and 61 Squadrons were tasked with destroying the targets and Gibson led his unit on the low-level daylight raid. Joining him on the raid were Flight Lieutenant John Hopgood and Pilot Officer David Shannon. It is also worth pointing out at this juncture, that Gibson's regular wireless operator was Pilot Officer Robert Hutchison, another man who would join him on the Dams raid.

In clear weather, Gibson attacked the power station at Montchanin from just 500 feet, claiming a direct hit with his bombs. He then flew back and forth while his crew machine-gunned the site. The German anti-aircraft defences reacted and Gibson would later note that his Lancaster received a few bullet holes, but the target was destroyed. One of Gibson's crew – navigator Pilot Officer Frank Ruskell – took a cine film of the operation and one of the stills was used for media propaganda stories.

The target Gibson attacked was not completely destroyed, but he had now completed his eighteenth operation with No. 106 Squadron.

Over the next few weeks, Gibson and his squadron made a number of attacks upon targets in Italy, but on 17 November, he was awarded the Distinguished Service Order (DSO). His citation stated:

> 'Since being awarded a bar to his Distinguished Flying Cross, this officer has completed many sorties, including a daylight raid on Danzig and an attack at Gdynia. In the recent attack at Le Creusot, Wing Commander Gibson bombed and machine-gunned the transformer station nearby from 500 feet. On 22 October 1942, he participated in a daylight attack on Genoa and, two days later, he led his squadron in a daylight sortie against Milan. On both occasions, Wing Command Gibson flew with great distinction. He is a most skilful and courageous leader whose keenness has set a most inspiring example.'

While there is no doubt about Guy Gibson's flying ability and his bravery, some might dispute whether he was leading just by example or bludgeoning his crews into action. As we have seen, he was not respected by everyone, but his senior commanders were undoubtedly overjoyed by the success and efficiency of his squadron.

Peter Stevenson was a teenage Warrant Officer in the Air Training Corps (ATC) and worked on various airfields in Lincolnshire during the war. In 1943, he was at RAF Syerston and assisted No. 106 Squadron's groundcrews. In an audio statement given to the International Bomber Command Centre in Lincoln he recalled his contact with Guy Gibson:

> 'Guy Gibson, he was a bighead and he had all sorts of funny ideas because he'd been a between wars officer, where at a time, social standing was very, very important and it was only towards the end of the war that Guy Gibson allowed himself to be photographed with his sergeant air crew. No. He would separate them out. In some of the early periods of the war, you don't see an NCO anywhere near him. All commissioned men. Guy did not approve of the ATC. He thought we were just a boys' club and wanted keeping clear of the real war, so we in general kept clear of him.'

One new crew, fresh out of the Heavy (Bomber) Conversion Unit, who felt the ire of Gibson was that of Pilot Officer Ronald Williams. This can be evidenced from his letters now held in the Imperial War Museum in London.

In October 1942, Ron Williams and his crew, joined Gibson's No. 106 Squadron from the Heavy Conversion Unit. The sergeant pilot was known as 'Buzz' Freeman and Ron Williams was the navigator. After a number of weeks training in November, during which time Gibson wanted to ensure they were up to scratch, they were sent on their first operational sortie to Turin on the twentieth. Unfortunately, the rear gun turret became unserviceable on their Lancaster and they had to return home early. As a new crew, Gibson and some of the others looked upon them with some suspicion, was this a case of LMF (Lack of Moral Fibre)?

In his letter home on 23 November, Ron Williams told his parents that they had found there to be a 'jinx' on their crew and it was now quite a joke when Freeman and his crew were due to fly. In addition to the flight to Turin, another sortie had been 'scrubbed' before they had even left the ground due to poor weather.

The crew did manage to fly one mission to Turin a few days later, but on the night of 9-10 December 1942, they returned early once again. In his letter home on 11 December, Ron Williams explained that their pilot Buzz Freeman had become sick and couldn't see his instruments. They turned back and with the help of the auto-pilot 'George' and the flight engineer (Sergeant Young), they managed to get home and land safely.

Upon landing there was, as Ron Williams put it, 'A lot of cross examination' and he had to sign a written statement detailing what had occurred during the flight. Buzz Freeman was taken to the Station Sick Quarters and the Medical Officer examined him the next day. Freeman was eventually placed before a medical board and Ron Williams noted in his letter home that it was certain he would never fly on operations again. Guy Gibson was less than impressed with the crew making yet another early return. (He had not been on the mission himself.)

Ron Williams told his parents how disheartening this was and the fact there was an official investigation. The rest of the crew tried to stick together and get another pilot, but Gibson sent the flight engineer to join another crew. Almost immediately a list of squadron crews was posted on the station noticeboard with Williams and his remaining crew mates listed as 'awaiting posting'. Guy Gibson's discipline and justice was certainly fast moving.

Williams told his parents that they had asked their new flight commander (believed to have been Dave Shannon, another favourite of Gibson and a man who would be on the Dambusters raid), what was going on? But he said he didn't know anything about it, so they were going to see the Wingco himself (i.e. Gibson).

It appears that despite the expeditious manner in which the crew was listed for posting, they remained on the airfield as non-operational, with the stigma of having LMF hanging over them. Was this part of Gibson's summary justice or was it just the Christmas holiday period which caused a delay? In wartime it is unlikely the Christmas period would have caused such a delay in posting and it may have been part of Gibson's summary punishment.

In another letter home to his parents on 30 December 1942, Williams told them that he had seen the adjutant that morning, but he thought the officer had forgotten all about them. Their bomb aimer was subsequently posted to an Operational Training Unit and Williams asked the adjutant if the rest of the crew were to be posted. The adjutant shockingly asked Ron Williams if he wanted to be posted? Their pilot, Buzz Freeman, was still on the base kicking his heels, attached to the Station Headquarters awaiting authority for a posting to Canada. (During the war there were many stories relating to aircrew alleged to have LMF. Often, they would be reduced in rank to a simple airman, ordered to undertake menial tasks and shunned by the other aircrews. Whether this occurred to Buzz Freeman in this case is not clear, but Ron Williams would retain his rank and continue flying.)

To be fair to Guy Gibson, there is some evidence that he could be a sympathetic commander. In his autobiography: *The Everlasting Arms*, John Searby recalls on page 186, that Gibson had humanity, stating he smoothed the exit of an officer older than he, who lacked the guts to fly. Where a lesser man would have made a fuss and flung the book at him, Guy said, 'Well, he's not bad really. He's a square peg in a round hole and it's not his fault he cannot face up to it. I'll fix it with the medics.'

The question is whether Gibson was being considerate to the man or removing an obstacle to his own success? Is it possible he was being considerate or was it because the man was an older officer and not a sergeant like Buzz Freeman?

As we shall see later in the book, there were other cases of crews or crew members being transferred away because of Gibson's belief they had failed the test of courage or did not meet his expected standards.

It is interesting to note how many people say that Gibson led from the front and was not an administrative commanding officer like so many others, many of whom stayed at home doing administrational matters. However, when the operations of No. 106 Squadron are examined in detail, there appears to be a different side to this.

During the three months, July to September 1942, No. 106 Squadron flew thirty-two raids, but Gibson flew on just twelve of these or 37.5 per cent of the total. In October and November 1942, the squadron flew twenty raids and Gibson flew on just eight of these or forty per cent of that total.

In December 1942, the squadron only flew six raids, another sixteen being cancelled due to the poor weather conditions.

Gibson did not fly on any of these six raids. Between January and 11 March 1943, when Gibson flew his last operation with No. 106 Squadron, the unit flew thirty-two raids, but he only took part in six of these or 18.8 per cent of the total.

Cumulatively over the ten months period July 1942 to March 1943, No. 106 Squadron flew ninety raids, but Gibson flew on just twenty-six of these (28.9 per cent). Of these, only fourteen were to targets in Germany, the others being in occupied France and Italy.

Guy Gibson was a brave man who had already completed two tours of operations, but this apparent reduction in the frequency of sorties may be due to enhanced administrative work and witness's memories being confused after so much time. In addition, there is the possibility that the Air Staff were telling him not to take part in so many operations, but this cannot be evidenced.

Gibson clearly had his favourites and one of those, as we have seen, was John 'Hoppy' Hopgood. Hopgood's flying logbook, held at the Imperial War Museum in London, is worth an examination. He was as we have seen, a very experienced pilot by late 1942 and when he completed his tour with No. 106 Squadron in October 1942, Gibson signed off his logbook with the comments:

> 'A very fine operational tour. This officer has pressed home his attacks with great determination and he has shown himself to be one of the most outstanding captains of No. 5 Group.'

John Hopgood was recommended for and awarded the Distinguished Flying Cross on 27 October 1942.

The following day, Gibson sent Hopgood a telegram congratulating him on his award (also held in the Imperial War Museum):

> 'Congratulations Hoppy glad to know you are completely rested, but you'll soon get out of that feeling when you are back here and know your new job – Wingco and the boys.'

Gibson was keen to reward skilful, brave pilots like John Hopgood, but was it fair to ostracise the rest of Buzz Freeman's crew?

In early December 1942, Guy Gibson met a 22-year-old RAF nurse named Corporal Margaret North at Rauceby Hospital, near Sleaford. He was visiting a number of his injured men when they became acquainted. Speaking in a BBC documentary called *Dambusters Declassified* in 2010 and also reported in the *Daily Mail* on 23 October that year, Margaret said:

> 'When I first met Guy, I'd gone out to help either operate on, or bring in a very badly injured officer. After kneeling on the floor for some time holding what was left of a badly injured arm, my knees rather hurt and I looked at a pair of legs behind me and said, "Can I borrow your legs to lean against?" I didn't know it at the time, but they were Guy's legs. That's how I first met him. My first impressions were that he was a typical officer – full of his own importance at times, but there was something about him that I wanted to know. And

> I did, he was charming. I found that he was in a bad spot, in fact his marriage was broken and he was lonely, unhappy, but he loved his job, everything was flying.'

The couple soon struck up a conversation and he asked her out for a drink. The two went on to become very close friends, taking secret long drives in the country side. They met in secrecy to avoid causing scandal, but according to Margaret, they lived in their own fantasy world, sharing a place they called Honeysuckle Cottage. Margaret told her BBC interviewer:

> 'Each meeting was adding a little bit to the cottage, I could tell you how many teaspoons we had. We did it that much. It was a form of escapism from the life we were leading, which on one hand was very dangerous and on my own behalf was very, very painful at times.'

The BBC interviewer asked if she thought Guy Gibson was in love with her? Margaret replied, 'I hope he was, yes, I was. – I'd be a fool if I wasn't.'

In the *Daily Mail* article, Margaret added that Guy could not confide in his wife, who was a former chorus girl and had little understanding of the demands of his military life.

Guy Gibson needed a pressure release and Margaret appears to have given him that. It appears on face value, that their contact was no more than platonic and a fantasy world. However, Margaret, in the *Daily Mail,* stated that cracks appeared in their relationship when Guy would not leave his wife.

Margaret was at the time already dating an RAF Sergeant (Douglas Fullins) and he proposed to her. Margaret told Gibson about the proposal, but his immediate reaction was not stated. He later reportedly telephoned her and pleaded with her not to marry the sergeant, but despite his desperate pleas, the wedding went ahead.

Although the two remained in contact, their meetings became less frequent. Eventually, she moved away from Gibson's airfield, and not surprisingly, Margaret does not get a mention in Gibson's book *Enemy Coast Ahead.*

In the summer of 1942, the poor accuracy of RAF bombing raids was addressed with the formation of a dedicated Pathfinder unit. The Luftwaffe had used a similar system using illuminating flares and the electronic Knickebein plotting/navigation device during the Blitz, so the RAF needed something similar but better.

We shall look at Pathfinder techniques later in the book, but in 1942 it is fair to say there was some initial scepticism regarding the idea. Gibson touched on this in his own book and recalled a mission to Saarbrücken, his first experience of the Pathfinders.

He described how they marked the inward flight path and then the target with target indicators and flares, before his own crew dropped their huge 8,000lb bomb. The next day they discovered the Pathfinders had mistakenly identified and marked the small town of Saarlouis, which had been obliterated by the main bomber force. A few nights later, the same thing happened again when Frankfurt was the target. This sounds like Gibson was not in favour of the Pathfinder Force, but in his next paragraph, he added that things started to improve under the command of Group Captain Don Bennett.

However, it was clear from his next comments that he was somewhat undecided about the accuracy and value of the Pathfinders (this comment being interesting as most of the book was written in the first few months of 1944).

In chapter fifteen of *Enemy Coast Ahead*, Gibson went into some detail regarding Pathfinder target marking and illumination techniques. Somewhat prophetically he mentions the introduction of the 250lb target marker (indicator) bomb and how it worked, bursting at about 3,000 feet and cascading down onto the target, hundreds of small red balls which burned for about five minutes, 'These were the bombs that put night bombing on the map,' Gibson stated.

On 15 October 1942, John Searby joined No. 106 Squadron as a flight commander. In his book *The Everlasting Arms*, he describes his first impression of Guy Gibson. Searby had been flying over the North Atlantic with few navigational aids, often in appalling weather conditions, it was dangerous and vital work, but it did not seem to impress Guy Gibson.

John Searby initially thought his new commanding officer to be abrupt and cocky. After discussing Searby's flying career up to that time, Gibson flippantly responded, 'You can forget all that, it means nothing, this is the real thing. Anything you may have done before you came here is nothing. This is the real thing.' Gibson walked to the office window, looked outside and said, 'Ops are what count here and anyone who doesn't like it can get out.'

On the face of it, this comment together with Gibson's earlier comments to Alex Kinnear and his crew about dying or getting a gong, appears arrogant and gung-ho. It was a less than friendly first meeting for John Searby and he admits he did not like him, but he had the intelligence to realise Gibson was under pressure the day after an operation in which three of his crews had failed to return.

John Searby would soon get to know Guy Gibson and gain a more favourable impression of him, but it is not difficult to see how many people could form a poor opinion of the man. Whereas Gibson appears to have formed instant impressions about people, others could have done the same with him.

Searby recalled that off-duty, Guy Gibson was all for a party, but he was also fatalistic, once telling him, 'They have little time left and might as well enjoy it.' This was a man who seemed to feel indestructible, but clearly, he had moments of fatalism, just like the time when his siblings presented him with a new watch for his twenty-first birthday.

On one occasion, Gibson showed Searby a new low-level bomb sight he was developing. He showed him the sight which a corporal had constructed, explaining how it worked. He even offered to take Searby with him on a test operation – something that Searby later admitted had filled him with dread.

The raids continued for Gibson and No. 106 Squadron, but on 10 January 1943, Major Richard Dimbleby, a BBC war correspondent arrived on the base. His role was to report on a bombing mission over Germany. Normally, Gibson would appear to have little time for such media people, but this time he was very welcoming and gracious. Whether this was because of orders from Bomber Command or his own liking of Dimbleby, who is said to have done everything he could to fit in, is unclear. There is also a third possibility, that Guy Gibson thought he might become a media star himself and he courted the limelight.

Less than a week later, on 16 January 1943, Gibson and his crew took the BBC man on a trip to the 'Big City' – Berlin. The sortie was anything but quiet for the correspondent. The flak over the capital of the Third Reich was its usual heavy self, but to make matters worse, the mid-upper gunner's heating system failed and the wireless operator, Robert Hutchison, went to assist him. Without an oxygen supply, Hutchison passed out and navigator Frank Ruskell went to his assistance. With Ruskell busy, they missed a turning point on the approach to the aiming point and Gibson took them round three times through the heavy flak, before they eventually dropped their bomb load.

During the course of this drama, Richard Dimbleby became sick, either through fear or air sickness, but he was certainly given the news story of his life. In his later report broadcast on BBC radio, Dimbleby reported that the crew were brave and exceedingly skilful airmen. He did not name the crew for obvious reasons, but he noted the 'Short, sturdy Wingco who had flown in every major raid of the war and been a night-fighter pilot.' Although Gibson's name was not in print or broadcast over the airwaves, everyone in Bomber Command who knew of Gibson, knew exactly who this individual was. It was clear Guy Gibson was 'Bomber' Harris's favourite commander and his star was still rising.

Gibson continued to fly on raids into February 1943 and he continued to make a name for himself with a flight to Milan. Although the Italian targets were not as well defended as those in Germany, they could still be deadly.

On this raid, Gibson circled the target longer than necessary, while his crew took a lengthy cine film of the raid. It almost appears as if Gibson thought he was immortal, continually circling around or over targets, or flying at low-level over well defended cities. This was not the first or the last time Gibson or his crew used a cine camera and he was an avid photographer. The cine camera was probably his own.

Gibson's last raid with No. 106 Squadron was to Stuttgart on 11 March 1943. As usual, he decided to break in a new pilot and took Flying Officer Walter Thompson with him for experience. As usual with a Gibson flight, the inexperienced Thompson certainly received an experience.

The Lancaster was not far into its journey to south-east Germany when the port outer Rolls-Royce Merlin engine failed. With a lengthy distance to Stuttgart over a very heavily defended area, Gibson could have ditched his bombs and returned home. However, this was to be his final operational flight before he went on leave and he did not want to make a further flight in a day or two. He therefore decided in characteristic style to crack on to Stuttgart, not at the same level as the bomber stream, but at low-level!

Many crews would have thought this suicidal, but the indestructible Wing Commander pressed onwards. What Thompson and the rest of the crew must have thought is probably unprintable, but they managed to dodge the bombs from the main bomber stream above them and returned home. The No. 106 Squadron Operations Record Book proclaimed that this was Gibson's last flight with the unit, undertaken on just three engines!

Guy went on leave to Cornwall and he received news that he had been awarded a bar to his Distinguished Service Order (DSO). He was now one of the most highly decorated pilots in the Royal Air Force, having completed three tours of operations. He was also something of a legend due to his low-flying skills, his willingness to loiter around a target or make repeated bombing runs. Negatively, he was also disliked by quite a number of people, but even they had to agree that he was a very fine, brave pilot and when the proverbial chips were down, an excellent leader.

Gibson was readily identifiable on the airfield, not only by his three wing commander stripes, but also wearing his Luftwaffe issue life jacket. He also took to leaving the top button of his tunic unbuttoned like a fighter pilot and he was always accompanied by his black labrador. Guy Gibson was certainly very different from the other bomber squadron commanders in early 1943.

Sheila Wilmet was a corporal in the WAAF based at Coningsby and attached to the meteorological unit. She recalled in an interview, now held by the International Bomber Command Centre in Lincoln and reproduced here with their kind permission:

> 'One of our fairly regular visitors was Group Captain (author's note: actually, Wing Commander) Gibson, and he would come in and ask the officer to explain the

> charts and what they meant, and what it would mean and how weather would travel etc. He was the only one that did that. The others would take whatever they were told at the briefing, but he liked to know the ins and outs of it. The down side of this visit was that he would quite often say as he looked down at his big black Labrador, "Oh, N***** would like some cocoa." I thought, oh dear. So away I'd have to go to the, well I wouldn't call it a kitchen. There was a kettle and I would do my best to make the cocoa. Make sure it wasn't too hot, come out and present it to N***** while others were talking weather wise. And then he would say, "Thank you. Come on N*****. You've had your treat."'

As a squadron commander Guy Gibson was the man who ensured things went well, he had to be direct and uphold discipline, but he could also be very sympathetic to individuals.

Bert Wigglesworth, who was part of No. 106 Squadron, remembered his CO visiting him in hospital after a flare had exploded in his hand. He was due to be married and when he left to go on leave, Gibson gave him and his new wife to be, a set of silver fish servers in a presentation case. A card was attached wishing the couple all the best for their future.

Guy Gibson had always tried to avoid throwing new crews directly into combat, until he or his flight commanders had checked their abilities. Staff at Group Headquarters were not too happy with this, but the short bombastic commanding officer was quick to tell them what he thought, before adding that his squadron's results spoke for themselves.

The morning after his last operational flight with No. 106 Squadron, Guy Gibson was woken by the adjutant. As he quickly came to his senses, he was told that he had to report to No. 5 Group Headquarters.

Chapter Four

Squadron 'X'

In *Enemy Coast Ahead*, Guy Gibson recalls telephoning Group Headquarters and speaking to the senior air staff officer. He was told John Searby would take command of No. 106 Squadron and Gibson was to attend Group Headquarters the following afternoon. The reason given for the summons was the Air Officer Commanding wanted Gibson to write a book for the benefit of new bomber pilots.

Guy Gibson naturally, was less than impressed, but he attended the headquarters as ordered. Before he departed his squadron, he asked the adjutant to send a telegram to Eve, telling her his leave was being cancelled. With such a strained marriage, this would not be the best of news for his distant wife in London. Despite this news, Gibson held a party that night at a nearby pub with a private function room to celebrate the end of his tour.

Upon arrival at No. 5 Group Headquarters at Grantham the following afternoon, Gibson was ushered in to see the Air Officer Commanding (AOC) – Air Vice-Marshal Ralph Cochrane.

The Air Officer Commanding congratulated his star squadron commander on completing yet another tour, before asking if he would do one more trip. Gibson asked what kind of trip it would be and Cochrane told him it would be a pretty important one, adding, 'Perhaps the most devastating of all time. I can't tell you any more now. Do you want it?' Gibson immediately agreed and left to await further orders.

Two days later, he was back at Grantham in front of Ralph Cochrane who was now joined by Air Commodore Charles Whitworth. The AOC explained that he could not tell Gibson what the operation was, but it could not be undertaken for at least two months. Gibson, in his own book, said he immediately thought of the *Tirpitz* battleship and wished he hadn't volunteered for the extra trip.

Gibson was told that Air Marshal Harris, the Commander-in-Chief of Bomber Command, had decided to form a special squadron of Lancasters and this would be stationed at Charles Whitworth's base at Scampton. Gibson stated in *Enemy Coast Ahead,* that he was told to pick the new squadron's crews – the best available and each squadron would be forced to surrender them to him.

Gibson was quick to request a number of pilots and their crews, he got the services of his long-time friend John Hopgood from No. 106 Squadron while snatching Dave Shannon, who was now at the Pathfinder Training Unit at RAF Warboys.

Although the Dambusters movie utilises Gibson's own written comments about hand-picking the crews himself, the reality was somewhat different. Not all the pilots were known personally to Gibson and over a third of them came from just two units: No. 57 and Gibson's last command – No. 106 Squadron. No. 57 Squadron supplied six pilots – the entire 'C' Flight of that unit commanded by Squadron Leader Henry 'Dinghy' Young DFC and bar, while along with Guy Gibson, there was John Hopgood, Dave Shannon and Flight Sergeant Lewis Burpee from No. 106 Squadron (Shannon having only recently transferred to the Pathfinder Training Unit).

The movie and Gibson himself, give the impression the pilots and crews were all assembled at once, Gibson briefing them in one large group. In *Enemy Coast Ahead*, Gibson says he got them altogether – a hundred and forty-seven men. They were quite young and he felt quite old (even at the age of twenty-four). He told them it was to be a special job, one that might cut short the duration of the war, but he warned them about security and discipline.

In reality, the crews arrived over a couple of weeks as their squadrons finally released them. In addition, the movie has one scene in the Officers' Mess at Scampton where the new arrivals are sharing a drink or two. One waiter tells another that he has never seen so many DFC medal ribbons on the new arrivals. Gibson also mentioned this incident in the Officers' Mess in his book and it is clear the movie takes a lead from his account in *Enemy Coast Ahead.*

The book is interesting, but has for many years been suspected of having a ghost writer. However, in the years before her death in late 1988, Eve Gibson was adamant her husband was its only author and there was no ghost writer. In addition, the original manuscript, which can still be read, contains various spelling and grammatical errors associated with Guy Gibson, some of which have been corrected by an editor or censor.

In *Enemy Coast Ahead,* Gibson reports there were a good number of Distinguished Flying Cross holders among the new arrivals, as well as a few Distinguished Service Orders. The

DFC was awarded either for a particular act, or more likely, at the end of a tour of operations. In reality, a good number of Gibson's new arrivals were still halfway or even less than halfway, through their first tour of operations; and some of the airmen in the various crews had not even flown one operation. Unlike the impression given by the book and the movie, most of the men had no decorations at all when they arrived at RAF Scampton.

While the movie and Gibson's own account in *Enemy Coast Ahead* can, in 2024, be seen as works of propaganda, in some ways the lack of experience among some of the crews is even more impressive, both for the personnel and their new commanding officer's efforts.

What is often overlooked by researchers and historians, is that Gibson was a hard task master and very quick to remove those he deemed unsuitable for the role. For example, three of the 'C' Flight crews from No. 57 Squadron were novices and not the experts Gibson wanted.

Pilot Officer Geoff Rice had less than a month's worth of combat experience, but Gibson kept him on the squadron. However, as we shall see, this man's experience of the Dams raid was anything but successful. Rice and his crew would remain on No. 617 Squadron until they were shot down in December 1943. Rice managed to evade capture for six months working with the resistance, but his crew were killed in the crash.

Flight Sergeant Raymond Lovell was sent back to No. 57 Squadron by Gibson because he was perceived to be too inexperienced and unlikely to make the specialist squadron's grade. However, not for the first time, Guy Gibson was found to be wanting in his initial assessment of a pilot. Raymond Lovell would survive the war as a Flying Officer, being awarded the Distinguished Flying Medal on 14 September 1943, less than four months after the Dams raid. The citation for his DFM noted that he had undertaken fifteen raids on the Ruhr and that:

> 'He has always evinced keenness for operational flying and pressed home his attacks with courage and determination. On the ground he has given valuable assistance in the training of his crew, which has been reflected in the successes attained.'

Flight Sergeant George Lancaster was another No. 57 Squadron pilot, but Gibson believed his navigator to be of a poor standard and needed to be transferred from the unit. Lancaster and the rest of the crew reportedly supported their colleague and demanded they be transferred away with their navigator. George Lancaster is also believed to have survived the war.

It appears that not only did Gibson make an incorrect assessment of these individuals, he also appears to have favoured officers over NCO's.

Gibson knew the forthcoming operation would require a sortie of continuous low-flying, something he enjoyed and he was keen to add Flight Lieutenant Harold 'Mick' Martin to his new squadron. The two men had previously met at an investiture at Buckingham Palace, where the Australian pilot had spoken of his own experience and knowledge of low-flying. As far as Gibson was concerned, Martin was the perfect man for his new unit.

While Guy Gibson had to sort out aircrew and new aircraft, there was also the issue of aircraft maintenance and general squadron administration. To assist him with this, Gibson quickly obtained the services of Flight Sergeant George 'Chiefy' Powell and Sergeant Jim Heveron, once again recruited from No. 57 Squadron. (Gibson must have been extremely unpopular with the unit's commanding officer!)

The two men were already at Scampton with No. 57 Squadron, so they were quickly assimilated into the new unit. Gibson told the two sergeants what he wanted and allowed the trusted NCOs to arrange everything. If they met resistance, they had only to speak with their new CO and he would do the rest in his own demanding and unremitting manner. Guy Gibson was a man who took no prisoners, he had been given an order from the top and he was determined to carry it out. If anyone or anything got in his way, he would remove it immediately.

Flight Sergeant George 'Chiefy' Powell took charge of discipline, he was an interesting character having been an air gunner on Nos. 500 and 57 Squadrons. He chose not to wear his air gunners brevet, which he was entitled to carry on his chest, explaining later that he didn't want the new aircrews to think he was one of them.

It has been reported over the decades, that a new unnamed adjutant was brought in to assist Gibson when the squadron was formed, but he allegedly fell victim to Gibson's impetuous demands and was soon replaced by Flight Lieutenant Harry Humphries from RAF Syerston. Gibson does not mention the initial adjutant in *Enemy Coast Ahead,* stating that they needed one and Charles Whitworth had Harry Humphries posted to them after a few days without an adjutant. There is no doubt throughout this book that Gibson as a commanding officer always had a number of flight commanders and in this case, senior ground staff and NCO's who he could trust to deliver his targets. As a leader and manager, he built a team and set standards which he expected to be attained. Anyone who failed to meet these standards was quickly dealt with and in a number of cases, removed from his elite unit.

It took some time to pull the unit together, but for a newly formed squadron, the pace was electrifying. The unit was eventually designated No. 617 Squadron, although the squadron badge would not be created and authorised by King George VI until after the forthcoming raid.

The Lancasters, when they arrived, were given the squadron code AJ and Gibson's personal aircraft was coded AJ-G. The letter 'G' clearly referred to Gibson's surname, but although it may have been a coincidence, the three letters of Gibson's aircraft were the initials of his father.

The preparations for the Dams raid and the attack itself have been the subject of many books, documentaries and magazine articles over the eighty-one years since 1943. This book is concerned with Guy Gibson as a character and his ultimate fate, so I shall not cover the raid in too much detail.

One element that has often been overlooked is Guy Gibson's relationship with the inventor of the Upkeep mine, otherwise known as the bouncing bomb – Barnes Wallis. The two men are said to have had a very good working relationship and in some ways the scientist was like a father tutoring a son. Gibson often visited Wallis at his home near Weybridge and regularly attended trials of the new bomb.

On, or just after 15 April 1943, Gibson attended trials near Reculver in Kent. The day before the trials he went in to Margate for fish and chips, but it would lead to another close shave with death. A flight of Focke Wulf 190's came out of the sun and bombed and strafed the crowded seaside resort with machine gun and cannon fire. Gibson was lucky to escape unharmed.

Attending the bomb trials was becoming dangerous work and on another visit to Kent, in a Miles Magister with his bombing leader Bob Hay, Gibson had to make a forced landing in a field full of anti-glider obstacles. Although Gibson and Hay survived with hardly a scratch, the Magister was wrecked by the obstacles.

Over the many decades that have passed since the Dams raid, a good number of people have left their views on the raid and in particular Guy Gibson. As we have seen, different people have different perspectives on Guy Gibson, depending on their experiences, their standing within the squadron, their rank and even their sex.

The Imperial War Museum holds a vast number of audio statements collected over many years and some of these, concern the contact individuals had with Gibson. The following statements have been provided to me by the archive to whom I am very grateful.

Sergeant Bill Townsend, in an audio statement recorded in 1984 said, 'I was a Sergeant at the time [he was with No. 617 Squadron] and I didn't know him socially in the Officers'

Mess, but he was a tough disciplinarian, he had things the way he wanted them. He insisted on a high standard. On the other hand, he was fun, he was never averse to a bit of fun in the Officers' Mess apparently, the boys [the officers] spoke very highly of him.'

Airman John Charles Elliott said, 'He seemed, what can you say? He seemed quite reasonable to me. I got to know him better when 617 was formed. I thought he was very fair and reasonable. He understood our problems and we tried to understand his.'

Eileen Mary Albone was a driver at Scampton and assigned to be Gibson's personal driver. One day they were near her parents farm and Gibson asked if she wanted to visit her mother. They attended the girl's home and Gibson had a cup of tea with her parents, before helping her father round up their sheep – Gibson opening and shutting gates for them. Eileen recalled, 'He was very good, he talked to me. He said, "Call me Guy." I said, "I can't do that, I'd call you Guy when we had the Group Captain in the car – I can't do that." He was always very friendly to me.'

Eileen was unmarried at the time and known as Eileen Strawson. In the *Grantham Journal* in 1993, she remembered an occasion near the airfield when they had hit and seriously injured a cockerel. Being a farm girl, she quickly put it out of its misery by wringing its neck, but Gibson was horrified to witness this and told her he did not know how she did it.

On another occasion, Eileen recalled it being very hot day when she collected Gibson in the car. He got in to the front and threw his service cap into the back seat. She told him she wished she could do the same and he told her to go-ahead and do it. She threw her cap into the back seat and they set off for Scampton. At the guardroom, Eileen stopped and entered to sign them both in, but she forgot to put her cap on. Inside the guardroom, the duty corporal put her on a charge. When she returned to the car and informed Gibson of this, he angrily went inside and told the corporal to *scrub* the charge against Eileen. The corporal was less than happy – he was only doing his job – and according to Eileen, he was thereafter always trying to get her on a charge of petrol misuse – without success.

Gibson's relationships with women is one that has often been subject of speculation. As we have seen, he was sent away to boarding school, his mother had died and his marriage to an older woman was somewhat strained by mid-1943. Clearly Gibson enjoyed being driven by Eileen and it appears had an easy-going, friendly relationship with her – something totally at odds with the disciplinarian's attitude towards the male members of his unit.

Gibson had enjoyed the company of the RAF nurse Margaret North, while also ensuring a WAAF officer, who had just lost her husband, was taken to the Officers' Mess and cared for. Gibson appears to have been happy to engage females in conversation and certainly in a very different manner to the way in which he spoke with Air Force friends and colleagues.

In many ways it is not hard to believe Guy Gibson was lonely and senior command has always been described as a lonely position. He distanced himself from ranks other than officers and his wife was living far away in London. His trusty black labrador was his constant and trusted companion, constantly breaking the rules by drinking in the Officers' Mess, urinating on the carpet and sleeping in Gibson's room and office. The dog was like the son Gibson would never have.

Even relationships with the officers appear to have been quite distant at times, with just a few close friendships like those with John Hopgood and Dave Shannon, his old companions from No. 106 Squadron.

Dave Shannon, who survived the war, was another who left an audio statement with the Imperial War Museum. He stated, 'Oh, he was an absolutely fantastic character in my own estimation, he was one of the finest leaders of men that I have ever met. He would never ask anyone to do anything he couldn't do or hadn't done himself. He was known as an operational squadron commander, that is to say, he flew just as many ops as his crew, which was not always the case with squadron commanders due to administrative work… He was very strict on duty and one of the boys off-duty.'

Gibson was in many ways a perfect senior officer and commander. Flying Officer Harold Sydney Hobday was a navigator with No. 617 Squadron and recalled in an audio statement, 'He was quite strict and wouldn't stand any nonsense, but he was very friendly. For instance, just before the raid, one of the chaps phoned his girlfriend, he wasn't supposed to you see; it was found out and he got a right telling off from Gibson. If anybody drank before going out on practice, he'd be down on them like a ton of bricks.'

Flight Sergeant Leonard J. Sumpter was a bomb aimer with No. 617 Squadron and said, 'He seemed like a nice little chap, he was short, broad shouldered, smart, I liked the way he walked about because he was smart, he didn't slouch about. He always looked well-dressed, trousers creased, a clean collar and well shaven. He was a driver, he was the sort who made people do things by example... If I can't do it, you can't do it, but if I can do it, you can do it.'

Guy Gibson clearly led by example and there have been a number of people who state it was a case of only doing things if he could do it, had done it before and if he believed it could be done. He would never ask anybody to do something he could not do himself.

However, there is no doubt he was driven by success, glory and decorations. As we have already seen, Flight Lieutenant Hugh Verity flew Beaufighters with Gibson on No. 29 Squadron and he mentioned the issue of decorations. This was repeated by Lawrence Wesley Curtis a wireless operator on No. 617 Squadron in another audio statement. Curtis said, 'When I first came before Guy Gibson he said, "I see you haven't got any decorations? That's surprising." I had a very good impression of him, I know some people think he was a bit hard, but I was very impressed. I got on very well with him, no problem. I found him likeable – hard, but very just. If he said do something, you did it, he had a very strong will and was a professional airman.'

In recent years before his death, Flight Sergeant 'Johnny' Johnson talked about his views on Guy Gibson in a YouTube video (titled: *Dambusters veteran Johnny Johnson, talks about Guy Gibson*). In the video, available on the website, he states, 'One of his, I would say short comings, was he could not bring himself down to the lower ranks in any way. He could communicate beautifully with senior officers above him and officer equals, and some as low as Flight Lieutenants; but he wasn't very good below that and with NCO's he didn't want to know. He was a keen disciplinarian, which didn't go down too well with NCO aircrew of course. He was OC of No. 106 Squadron at Syerston. I have to be very careful how I word this, but we were told he was known as the "Arch – born out of wedlock" by the crews there.'

'Johnny' Johnson went on to highlight how demanding Gibson was, not just to his crews, but to everyone. He recounted how, according to one story, Gibson refused almost petulantly to move from his office until the Air Ministry and Bomber Command gave him what he wanted for the squadron. Eventually, he got his way and carried on as if nothing had happened.

Johnson recalls that Gibson's leadership came on the raid itself when he repeatedly flew alongside other Lancasters as they made their bombing runs on the Möhne Dam. Johnson said this meant, 'I'm doing this, you're doing this, we're doing this together' and that in his opinion is the essence of good leadership.

This mantra about leading by example and from the front, comes through time after time in accounts about Gibson. He may have been remote with some people, a perfectionist and a man who cracked the proverbial whip, but when the chips were down, he would lead from the front and he has to be respected for this.

One element that has often been ignored is the stress associated with creating, managing and leading the new squadron. In *Enemy Coast Ahead,* Gibson himself describes how he started to get ill, irritable and bad-tempered. This soon included a 'carbuncle' which appeared on his face where he placed his oxygen mask and gout in his feet. Gibson went to see the Medical Officer who ordered two weeks rest, but there was no rest for Gibson and he carried on regardless of the doctor's orders.

The stress of creating a new specialised squadron and the required training, must have been very tough for Gibson and he continually relied upon the companionship of his four-legged friend as a stress relief. The dog had been with Gibson since his time at West Malling two years before and he was a welcome distraction. Gibson would take him for long walks around the airfield perimeter track, allowing him to de-clutter his mind. When he could not make time to walk the dog himself, Gibson would order an airman to take him outside.

The canine companionship sadly came to an abrupt end on the day of the Dams raid. The black Labrador who wandered freely around RAF Scampton, ran out of the main gate and onto the public road. He was hit and killed instantly by a car which failed to stop, although some people have disputed the element of failing to stop. Group Captain Charles Whitworth, the Scampton base commander, broke the terrible news to Guy and he was naturally distraught.

In *Enemy Coast Ahead*, Gibson recounts the tragedy stating, 'And so I went back to my room on the eve of this adventure with my dog gone – the squadron mascot. I was alone in my room looking at the scratch marks on the door he used to make when he wanted to go out, and feeling very depressed.'

Gibson kept the dog's death a secret, because he did not want the crews to think it a bad omen. In *Enemy Coast Ahead*,

Gibson says he asked Flight Sergeant 'Chiefy' Powell to bury his dog at midnight, when they would be crossing the enemy coastline. He added, 'While he was being buried, I hoped that we would be going over to give his friendly little soul an uplift with the job we were about to do.'

The lines are somewhat poetic and it would appear out of character for Gibson, but they indicate just how much his dog meant to him. The comment was indicative of two things, Gibson's religious upbringing and education, as well as his deep fondness for his constant companion.

With just a few hours to go until they took off on the historic raid, Guy Gibson had lost his beloved dog who had been his constant companion since his time at West Malling. In addition, his marriage to Eve was on the rocks. He was not close to many people, he was tired, stressed and in many ways alone with his thoughts, but despite this, he had to keep going and lead the attack on the dams.

In her book *Dambuster,* Susan Ottaway describes how Guy Gibson reacted to the death of his dog and how much he meant to him. Gibson allegedly went to the station workshop and asked a flight sergeant to make a wooden coffin for the dog's burial. The sergeant, who was probably very busy with the impending raid, refused to assist his commanding officer and an argument ensued between the two men. Despite his senior rank, Gibson did not get his way and the dog was buried without a coffin. This account displays the deep loss Guy must have felt, but it also perhaps shows him to be fallible and the death to have distracted him from his mission. It is also possibly indicative that the sergeant had little time for his senior officer's loss, perhaps due to the CO's previous attitude towards those who did not hold the King's commission?

The Labrador was buried as directed, by Flight Sergeant 'Chiefy' Powell on the grass verge outside Gibson's office window attached to the No. 617 Squadron hangar. A marker stone with an inscription would later be placed on the grave after the raid. The dog remains there to this day, although there have been recent attempts and consideration in moving the grave now that the RAF has vacated Scampton in 2023.

The Dams raid was a great success, the Möhne and the Eder dams were breached while the Sorpe was slightly damaged, but it came at a very high price.

Gibson was the first to attack the Möhne Dam, flying through numerous lines of anti-aircraft tracer as they arched over and beyond his Lancaster. Having successfully dropped his Upkeep mine, Gibson stood off the target and watched, hoping the wall of the dam would roll over under the pressure of the water. The dam held firm. They waited about ten minutes for the surface of the water to calm down and then Gibson called in his close friend and old No. 106 Squadron colleague – John 'Hoppy' Hopgood to attack.

Hopgood closed in on the Möhne Dam and was hit by flak in an inboard fuel tank, a sheet of flame streaming back from the ruptured fuel tank. The mine was dropped, but it bounced over the top of the dam and struck the power station in the valley below, exploding shortly afterwards in a vivid flash. John Hopgood's Lancaster, which probably received further damage from the exploding power station, struggled onwards with its pilot making a brave attempt to gain height to allow his crew to bale out, but it was no use; there was another vivid flash and the aircraft disintegrated before Gibson's eyes. His dog had gone and now his closest friend 'Hoppy' Hopgood had also left this world.

Gibson paused momentarily to take stock of the situation. Despite his own losses that day, he continued to conduct the attack and flew alongside the following Lancasters, attempting to draw anti-aircraft fire away from them as they dropped their mines on the Möhne Dam. Eventually, the Möhne cracked and the wall collapsed, sending a great torrent of water down the valley and through the villages, towns, airfields and factories. Robert Hutchison, Gibson's wireless operator sent the code word confirming their success at the Möhne Dam… the word was N-----, the name of Guy's beloved Labrador.

Having dropped their mines, Gibson sent 'Mick' Martin and Dave Maltby home, while he took the other crews on to the Eder Dam. There they repeated the destruction, but the American Joe McCarthy and Joe Brown failed to breach the Sorpe Dam.

The surviving Lancasters quickly headed for home and Gibson's rear gunner, Richard Trevor-Roper, spotted an unidentified aircraft behind them. Gibson hugged the ground and they managed to lose it in the pre-dawn darkness of the earth and some mist.

When they landed at Scampton and headed to the intelligence debriefing, Gibson was met by Air Marshal Arthur Harris and the No. 5 Group AOC – Air Vice-Marshal Ralph Cochrane. An official RAF photographer was on scene to capture the moment for publicity purposes and is reproduced in the image section of this book.

Gibson was soon informed of his squadron's losses. As well as losing John Hopgood and his crew, Squadron Leader Henry 'Dinghy' Young and his crew were missing (shot down and killed by flak on the way home over Holland). Henry Maudsley and his crew were also missing. Flight Lieutenant Bill Astell and his crew had crashed after hitting power lines, as had Flight Lieutenant Barlow and his crew. Sergeant Byers and his crew had also been shot down over Holland.

Pilot Officers Lewis Burpee and Warner Ottley and their crews were shot down on the way home, the only survivor from the two crews being Flight Sergeant Frederick Tees.

The No. 57 Squadron novice Pilot Officer Geoffrey Rice, who Gibson had kept while sending his NCO colleagues back to their unit, clipped the sea on the way out to the target and lost his mine and two engines. He immediately returned home, but Gibson is said to have commiserated with him rather than admonishing him. Was this a reflection of the losses that night and their effect upon Gibson, or was this yet more evidence of him being sympathetic with Rice because he was an officer?

This accusation appears to gather credence when one considers the other pilot who did not attack the dams. That pilot returned to Scampton without having dropped his mine, he was Flight Sergeant Cyril Anderson. He had become hopelessly lost, knocked off track by the searchlights and flak, he failed to locate the target. With dawn fast approaching, Anderson and his crew headed home before the night-fighters could find them.

In a repetition of the incident with Ron Williams and his crew on No. 106 Squadron in December 1942, Cyril Anderson was questioned at length by Guy Gibson, who was less than impressed. Bringing bombs back was almost a *capital offence* in Gibson's eyes and he informed the sergeant he would be transferred to another squadron with his crew as soon as possible. Within a few weeks, Flight Sergeant Cyril Anderson, who came from a working-class background in Wakefield, was transferred back to his original unit – No. 49 Squadron. He would be killed four months later on a raid to Mannheim on 23 September 1943, having completed thirteen operations.

It is interesting to note, that despite Anderson being admonished and transferred away from No. 617 Squadron and the comments that Gibson did not like having his photograph taken with NCO aircrew; the two men were photographed together with the other surviving aircraft captains on the steps of the Officers' Mess in an official image. This image is also contained within the photographic section of this book.

Guy Gibson must have been shocked by the losses – eight Lancasters had been lost together with their crews, a total of fifty-six men (however, Gibson did not know at the time, that three men had survived to become prisoners of war).

The following night a great party was held at Woodhall Spa and the unit was inundated with congratulatory messages. The BBC announced the raid as a great success that afternoon and aerial reconnaissance photographs were soon published in the newspapers to show the devastation the Dambusters had caused.

Although the aircraft returned around dawn, Guy only telephoned Eve that afternoon after she had heard the BBC announcement. In later years, she would recall that Guy did not seem too interested in discussing the raid. Perhaps he was still concerned with the unit's losses or he was concerned about security, knowing that the telephones were still being intercepted and checked.

Sergeant Jim Heveron was responsible for typing up the fifty-six letters, telling the families their loved ones were missing. Gibson would sign these in due course and as always, he would add in his own hand writing, a few more personal comments, something he had done with No. 106 Squadron.

Whether he wanted it or not, Guy Gibson was about to become a famous celebrity and public property. His life would change forever and what he did not know at the time, was his current Air Force career and operational flying were coming to an abrupt end.

In due course, once the letters had been signed and the celebrations completed, Gibson made an entry in his flying logbook. This noting that his total number of flying hours now stood at 1,924 hours and 20 minutes. A short time later, he would add simply and somewhat modestly in block capital letters: 'AWARDED VC.'

Chapter Five

The Fallout from the Dams Raid

The list of well-wishers sending congratulatory telegrams to Guy Gibson and his squadron was long and distinguished. The Chief of the Air Staff Sir Charles Portal, the Secretary of State for Air Sir Archibald Sinclair and Lord Trenchard, the so-called father of the Royal Air Force, all sent their congratulations, as well as Air Marshal Arthur Harris and Air Vice-Marshals Ralph Cochrane and John Slessor.

The raid had been a huge morale booster for the beleaguered British people. Newspapers were quick to take up the story of how an elite squadron of Lancasters had breached the great dams of Nazi Germany. The Royal Air Force rarely named individuals, even top scoring fighter aces who were treated differently to their American allies and those in Germany, but Gibson's name appeared in the headlines.

Guy Gibson DSO and bar, DFC and bar, was now the nations' biggest wartime hero and public property. He did not realise it at the time, but this would soon prevent him from remaining with 'his boys' and No. 617 Squadron.

Despite the public and media adulation, Gibson entered a period of self-reflection and in many ways depression. He had lost a high number of men and some very good friends. He had lost his faithful dog and his marriage was strained to the point of breakdown. Despite this strain, Gibson took a weekend leave with Eve at her parent's home in Penarth. He was hailed as a national hero wherever he went, but inside he was still grieving.

The Prime Minister, Winston Churchill, was quick to heap praise on the young pilot and his squadron of heroes. In just over ten days, the new celebrity would be awarded Britain's highest military honour – the Victoria Cross. Arthur Harris personally telephoned Gibson in Penarth to give him the good news.

The award citation was detailed and informed the nation of Guy Gibson's operational career to date. It stated he was an operational bomber pilot who had established a reputation as an outstanding pilot. He made a number of single-handed attacks on his 'rest' nights, against heavily defended targets which included the battleship *Tirpitz* in Wilhelmshaven. After he had completed his tour on bombers, 'He asked for a further operational posting and went to a night-fighter unit instead of instructional duties.' There, he destroyed at least three enemy bombers and contributed to the raising and development of the new night-fighter formations.

The citation continued stating that a further tour on bombers followed and when that concluded, Gibson had pressed strongly to remain on operations. He was selected to command a new squadron formed for special tasks and under his inspiring leadership, the squadron had executed one of the most devastating attacks of the war. The citation went on:

> 'The task was fraught with danger and difficulty. Wing Commander Gibson personally made the first attack on the Möhne dam. Descending to within a few feet of

> the water and taking the full brunt of the anti-aircraft defences, he delivered his attack with great accuracy. Afterwards he circled very low for thirty minutes, drawing the enemy fire upon himself, in order to leave as free a run as possible to the following aircraft which attacked the dam in turn. Wing Commander Gibson then led the remainder of the force to the Eder dam where, with complete disregard for his own safety, he repeated the tactics, and once more drew upon himself the enemy fire so that the attack could be successfully developed. Throughout his operational career, prolonged exceptionally at his own request, he had shown leadership, determination and valour of the highest order.'

This was high praise for the nations' new hero. Despite being awarded the Victoria Cross Guy was very downhearted. Eve would later state that he was very subdued and spoke only of the loss of John Hopgood and the others. Like many others who survive a tragic event and are hailed as heroes, he felt almost guilty to have not only survived, but to have received the Victoria Cross.

After his weekend leave, Gibson returned to Scampton and on 27 May, HM King George VI and Queen Elizabeth visited the airfield. Gibson, although apparently still somewhat downhearted, put on a brave face and performed dutifully for the royal visitors and the attendant media cameras. A large number of black and white and colour images were taken at the event, many of them concentrating on Gibson as he escorted his royal guests and introduced them to the aircrews and other officers. The royal party and Gibson moved on to view the target models used to brief the aircrews and one of the Lancasters used on the raid.

Gibson had been informed of the award of his VC before the official announcement was made in the *London Gazette*. Impatient to have the nation's highest honour placed on his uniform, he had the famous crimson ribbon sewn onto his tunic alongside his DSO and DFC by a WAAF. This caused a little consternation during the royal visit, as the award was not yet public knowledge and when he was photographed with the King and Queen, the VC ribbon was proudly on display to the worlds media. The media were quick to identify the famous medal ribbon on the new hero's tunic and it had to be explained away by the Air Ministry media department as an innocent error! But in reality, the new hero had breached protocol, nothing new for Guy Gibson.

A large number of other members of No. 617 Squadron were also awarded a variety of decorations and they were all listed in the unit's Operations Record Book.

Shortly after the visit of the King and Queen, Gibson headed north to Sheffield on an official visit. He was interviewed by the local media at a *Wings for Victory* event and he was overcome by the adulation and attention he received from the towns people. In London, Eve, the new hero's wife, was interviewed by the media and asked a variety of questions about her husband. She was even interviewed on camera and appeared on the various news reels in cinemas across the nation.

Despite the strain on his marriage, Guy still wanted it to succeed and he wanted a home for his wife Eve near the airfield at Scampton. However, this was against the current RAF policy, which forbid wives to live within a certain distance of their husband's base. This apparent refusal by Guy to even consider Bomber Command's domestic policy, seems to indicate that he was possibly 'getting above his position in life.' Why should he be allowed to live with his wife near the air base, when other junior aircrew members were forbidden? It would also be difficult for Eve to be the only wife around – something she allegedly pointed out to Guy when he informed her of his plans. There is however, another possibility – that Gibson knew his operational flying days were over and he was to be grounded.

Behind the scenes at the Air Ministry, there was debate about what to do with No. 617 Squadron and their commanding officer, now the Dams raid was over. Could they be used for other specialist raids or should they be disbanded and the crews distributed to other squadrons?

While the Air Ministry debated the future of Gibson's squadron, he continued on his numerous publicity appearances across the nation.

On Sunday, 19 June, Guy Gibson returned to one of his favourite places – Kent. He visited the 1st Tovil Scouts in Maidstone after an invite from Glad Bincham, whom he knew from his time at West Malling and made a short speech to the youngsters, extolling the virtues of being a scout above those of the Hitler Youth. Although, as a boy he had only been a scout himself for a very short period of time, Gibson was keen to point out that he knew scouting would give them all the skills they needed for service in the armed forces. The speech was caught on camera and presented in cinema news reels across the nation, Guy's star was reaching its peak of ascendency. He was made an honorary member of the Tovil Scout Troop, before being driven in the open back of a lorry through the streets of Maidstone, where massed crowds applauded and cheered the nation's new national hero.

On Monday, 20 June, Guy Gibson, accompanied by his wife Eve, attended Buckingham Palace with the other squadron members due to be decorated. Once again, the free worlds' media were in attendance and numerous photographic images and news film reels were recorded of the event.

Later that night, the manufacturers of the Lancaster bomber – A.V. Roe, threw a large party for the squadron at the Hungaria restaurant in Lower Regent Street and the aircraft's chief designer, Roy Chadwick, attended. Gibson was reportedly at the centre of the partying, which went on late into the night and there were various hijinks, the like of which would normally be frowned upon, but this was after all, the Dambuster party.

It was now over a month since the raid and the squadron were pretty much still on leave. Prime Minister Winston Churchill had been keen to push the propaganda value of the Dams raid, especially for the American audience and Air Marshal Arthur Harris was content for Gibson and the squadron to be paraded for the world's media. Harris believed this showed *his* bombing strategy was working and destroying the German war industry. He therefore continued to push for more strategic bombing of the German cities, believing bombing alone could win the war. If the Americans could bomb by day and the British and their Commonwealth allies by night, Arthur Harris firmly believed Germany could be brought to her knees.

Although most historians acknowledge that 'Bomber' Harris was happy to utilise Gibson's visit to North America, in his foreword to Gibson's 1946 autobiography *Enemy Coast Ahead,* he declares that he had to enforce a rest upon Gibson. He says he made a personal appeal to Winston Churchill to take Gibson with him, arranging for him to be detained on the other side of the Atlantic touring air bases and giving talks to airmen. Churchill (as we shall see shortly), summoned Gibson to his country residence at Chequers.

At the start of July 1943, Gibson returned to Scampton and his squadron, but he was effectively grounded, at least operationally. Despite this directive, on the second day of the month he made a low-level flight to Cornwall and back.

No. 617 Squadron were now effectively commanded by Guy Gibson in name only. His two flight commanders, Dave Maltby and the newly arrived Squadron Leader George Holden, managed the squadron and in July, the unit conducted three raids without Gibson to Italy and North Africa.

While the squadron undertook these operations, Gibson was required to attend a series of meetings considering the risk of similar retaliatory raids against British dams. (Unknown to the British at that time, the German's had recovered an undetonated Upkeep mine from the raid, but they were still trying to understand how it operated.) In addition, consideration was being given to using the Upkeep mines for a number of raids on other dams and similar targets, even against large capital ships such as *Tirpitz.*

On 24 July 1943, Gibson and Eve were invited to visit Churchill at Chequers for luncheon. Churchill who used to regularly sit alone and watch news films, sat with his guests and watched a number, including one on the subject of the treatment of Jews in Germany and Europe. Gibson was reportedly shocked and appalled at what he had seen, the material making him want to return to operations as soon as possible.

That evening, Gibson visited Sir Charles Portal at the Air Ministry in London. The Chief of the Air Staff was about to depart with numerous other officials and Winston Churchill to visit North America. This was for the Quebec Conference – code named Quadrant. US President Franklin D. Roosevelt, Churchill and the Canadian Premier William MacKenzie King would all be in attendance with their senior military commanders and politicians such as Anthony Eden. Gibson was informed by Sir Charles Portal, that Winston Churchill wanted him to accompany the British contingent to North America.

It has been claimed that the accompanying Guy Gibson was just a propaganda stunt, but in reality, it was to show the Americans that the British bomber offensive was the way forward. Many in the United States believed the bombing offensive was not very effective and the 8th US Army Air Force had been suffering significant losses during its daylight raids without long-range fighter protection. Harris, who wanted more bombers for his strategic bombing plan, believed the strategy needed unwavering public support from Roosevelt and the others; and Gibson could push that along by a series of public appearances and speeches. Whether he knew it or not, Guy Gibson had gone from an operational squadron commander to war hero and now he was a propaganda and political tool. The possibility of his return to combat operations and his beloved No. 617 Squadron was diminishing by the hour.

On Monday, 2 August 1943, Gibson made his last flight with his Dams raid crew. They flew yet another non-operational cross-country flight, but this one had Squadron Leader George Holden on board as a second pilot. It is believed to have been a similar flight profile to their Dams raid practice flights, flown over a number of lakes, reservoirs and dams to show George Holden the proverbial 'ropes'.

On Tuesday, 3 August, Gibson handed over command of *his* unit to the newly promoted George Holden. Gibson's crew would now fly with their new commanding officer.

Gibson told Eve he was going away and would be overseas for some time. Whether he actually divulged what his destination was is unknown, but he travelled by train to Glasgow. The following day, he joined Winston Churchill and his entourage on board the RMS *Queen Mary* – the *Grey Ghost,* as the German navy called her and set sail for Halifax, Nova Scotia. The ship sailed at full-speed, carrying a who's who of the British political and military establishment, including Lord Louis Mountbatten.

The *Queen Mary* docked in Halifax on 10 August and Guy Gibson escorted his Prime Minister to a number of official luncheons, where he was presented to the Canadian Premier and other dignitaries. Once the official luncheons and meetings were over, Gibson started a series of public presentations in Canada where he spoke about the strategic bombing campaign. The media asked him about his experience of Canadian aircrew which he naturally said impressed him, before he moved on to a series of visits to RCAF air bases and training establishments. Guy performed perfectly, always saying the right things and never inviting controversy. It must be assumed he was fully briefed, but he still had to perform and perform he did.

Within days of arriving, Guy Gibson had visited a number of Canadian cities, towns and air bases. He then diverted to New York at the request of Churchill, where the American media were waiting to interview this new hero of the air.

In the Harris papers held at the RAF Museum, Hendon, there is a short memorandum addressed to Air Marshal Harris dated 14 August 1943. It states that Air Commodore Blackford, Air Attaché to Washington DC, has asked if Wing Commander Gibson can stay in the United States after his duties with the Prime Minister are over. This was to take part in a film called, '*Episodes of Allied Air Forces*' and was being made by Harold Hawkes the American film producer. A British episode would cover the Dams raid, a lot of non-sensitive material having already been supplied by the Air Ministry and the RAF, as it was to assist in propaganda. It was felt Gibson's appearance in the film would enhance the propaganda value enormously. A pencil note made on the memorandum merely states, 'Spoken Peck', which probably refers to Sir Richard Peck at the Air Ministry. What that discussion entailed is unknown, but the Hawkes film was never made.

Various written articles detailing Gibson and the raid soon followed, some attributed to Gibson himself, but this cannot be confirmed and some are believed to have been the work of the famous writer Roald Dahl. Dahl was the Assistant Air

Attaché in Washington DC at the time and a former fighter pilot, having served in Greece during 1940–41. During his time in Washington, Roald Dahl was regularly writing and he may have been the ghost writer for some of these articles.

Gibson was soon back in Canada and heading westwards to Calgary and Moose Jaw on his long tour. The meetings, presentations and interviews were continuous and very repetitive, but Gibson maintained his professional composure and continued, smiling his way through the continuous throng of admirers.

Although the official reports state this extended tour was a success, there is one audio statement held by the International Bomber Command Centre in Lincoln, which gives a slightly different account with an unreported incident.

William Bullock was a former Flight Lieutenant and Engineering Officer at East Kirkby in 1944. He was also a former Halton Apprentice from 1932. In his audio statement, Bullock recalls Guy Gibson arriving at RAF East Kirkby in 1944 and a rumour from that time of an incident in Canada. He said:

> 'Guy Gibson, when he'd done his job, he came to us at East Kirkby for a rest. And he wasn't a nice man. A very unpopular man. "Don't call me Guy. Call me 'Dambuster'", he used to say. In Canada he was getting a bit too familiar with some bloke's wife. A great big Dutchman he was, so he just went up and he dropped him. "THUNK!" He said, "Leave my wife alone." He (Gibson) wasn't a popular man at all.'

We have no corroboration for this story, but the comment about calling him 'Dambuster' does resonate with other reports of his arrogance and a bombastic attitude.

In mid-September 1943, Gibson arrived in Calgary and made time to meet with Leading Aircraftsman Robert Young. He was the younger brother of Henry 'Dinghy' Young, killed on the Dams raid. He also met with the mother of his Dams raid navigator – Mrs Taerum – twice during his time in Calgary, the two talking for quite some time.

Sadly, the hand of fate decreed that soon afterwards, on the night of 15-16 September, her son, together with fellow dams crew members Frederick Spafford, Robert Hutchison and George Deering, would die with their CO and Gibson's successor George Holden, on a raid to the Dortmund-Emms Canal. It took four days for the news to reach Canada and by the time news arrived, Gibson had moved on to other appointments in Montreal.

When exactly Gibson was told of the loss of his crewmen is unknown and his feelings also appear to have gone unrecorded, but on 20 September, in Montreal, Gibson perhaps let his mask slip. Whether it was due to fatigue or depression brought about by the loss of his crewmen, he appears to have dropped his guard and spoken candidly about the strategic bomber offensive and its morality. In a speech, Gibson openly questioned the ability of Bomber Command to knock Germany out of the war with bombing alone. The speech in front of an audience which contained a number of very senior officers, differed from what would become Harris's own mantra – the belief that area and saturation bombing of German industrial centres would lead to that nations defeat.

In October 1943, Gibson arrived in Washington DC to be honoured by the United States Government with the prestigious Legion of Merit. It was rare for a Briton to receive this American award and only two others at that time had received it. In fact, it was rare due to an agreement between the two nations, for any Briton to receive any American award at the time. This was to prevent duplication and confusion, but Guy Gibson was being given a very high honour by the United States of America. He was photographed in colour, wearing the new medal ribbon and a set of USAAF pilots wings on his left breast, opposite his RAF wings and his British medal ribbons.

Gibson continued the seemingly endless tour with Chicago, Pittsburgh and a number of other cities being visited. He ended up in Los Angeles and Hollywood where he was again feted, this time by the glamourous and glitzy movie world. A move on to San Francisco concluded the American element of this tour and he eventually flew back to Ottawa in Canada.

On 1 December 1943, the tour finally concluded and Gibson was flown by long-range B-24 Liberator from Montreal to Prestwick in Scotland. The North American tour had been an enormous success, especially for the British political establishment and Gibson had been a sensation, but Guy was now further away than ever from operational flying.

Soon after his return, Gibson was debriefed at the Air Ministry in London, but the long tour had left him exhausted and he desperately needed a rest. The continuous public appearances, speeches and travelling had left him drained, so drained and thin, he had been operating on adrenalin in the final weeks of the tour.

After arriving in London, Gibson went to the house in Aberdeen Place, St. John's Wood where Eve lived. She was reportedly shocked by his thin, gaunt appearance, but he had no sooner arrived home, than he left for his old base at Scampton. He arrived at his air force home expecting to find 'his' 617 Squadron in residence, but they were now at Coningsby. Desperate to see his old colleagues, he telephoned Coningsby and requested a car drive over to Scampton to pick him up.

When he arrived at the Officers' Mess at Coningsby, Gibson was somewhat disappointed to find very few of the old faces from May 1943. Dave Shannon, Joe McCarthy and Harold 'Mick' Martin were still on the squadron, but he knew his successor, Wing Commander George Holden and a number of his old crew had been killed in September on a raid to the Dortmund-Ems Canal near Nordhorn.

After meeting his old colleagues and having a few drinks in the Officers' Mess, during which the new commanding officer, Wing Commander Leonard Cheshire, kept out of the way, Gibson went to the No. 5 Group HQ to try and get a new command from Air Vice-Marshal Ralph Cochrane. Unfortunately for Gibson, he was deemed to be too weak and tired for operations, and placed sick by the senior command. In addition, he was now identified as a war criminal by the Nazi regime and Adolf Hitler had reportedly put a price on his head – he was just too valuable to be put on operations.

In January 1944, Gibson, still weak and unfit for flying, was posted to a staff role on the Directorate of Accidents in the Air Ministry. He was also asked once again, to write his biography – a book which would ultimately become *Enemy Coast Ahead.*

The book took many weeks and months of writing and it was probably something Gibson would not have completed without the direction and request of the authorities, but he did what he was ordered. The original draft of the book is something of a surprise to many people when they read it. The book, which is held in the RAF Museum, Hendon, which was stringently edited and censored, contains a series of derogatory comments about various people, from members of his own crew to politicians, senior commanders and even people in certain professions and geographical locations around the nation. Most of these comments were deleted from the first published version in 1946. In many ways it shows the real non-public face of Guy Gibson in 1944.

Although Eve Gibson would always maintain the book was written solely by her husband, many people who knew him, found it hard to believe he could be so elegant with his writing. Although the censors and editors later altered some of the content and undoubtedly corrected the grammar and spelling, the general thread remained the same. It is therefore surprising when one reads the book today to find Gibson stating, 'To the following pilots and their crews who fought with me against our enemy,' before listing the captains of aircraft lost throughout his time on Nos. 83, 29, 106 and 617 Squadrons.

Finally, he states, 'AND MY CREW missing night September 15, 1943,' before listing Spafford, Taerum, Hutchison, Deering and Trevor-Roper, together with their nicknames. These comments were incorrect and misleading. Pulford was not listed, even though he had died a month before Trevor-Roper, who had actually died in 1944, not in 1943.

We know Gibson's crew were not all killed that night. George Holden and his crew, which consisted of Spafford, Deering, Taerum, Hutchison and two others, died over the Dortmund-Ems Canal near Nordhorn. This was therefore only two thirds of Gibson's Dams raid crew and Trevor-Roper and Pulford, the latter not even being listed, were killed with separate crews in February and March 1944.

The question is whether these errors and omissions were due to the editors or did Guy Gibson believe his entire crew were on board Holden's Lancaster that night in 1943? And what happened to John Pulford his flight engineer? Why did Gibson not even mention him? Sadly, it is a question only Guy Gibson can answer, but it is interesting to note that in the original uncensored draft of *Enemy Coast Ahead*, it is clear he had a very poor opinion of his flight engineer, stating he was dull and incapable of independent thinking. This is very unfair, but in Gibson's estimation, clearly Pulford did not reach the lofty heights of Hopgood, Shannon and others.

Even Flight Sergeant George Deering was described as 'Pretty dumb' in the initial draft, but this was later changed to 'Pretty green' in the published version. In reality, Deering was anything but green, having undertaken over thirty operational sorties by May 1943. Were these comments and omissions about the only two NCOs in his crew more indicative of Guy Gibson as a person than errors?

In February 1944, Guy Gibson had recovered sufficiently to undertake further public appearances. He was a very busy man and the public adored him.

Guy Gibson had previously met and become friends with Garfield Weston, a Canadian and Conservative, Member of Parliament for Macclesfield in Cheshire in 1943. By 1944, Weston was looking for someone to replace him as an MP and Guy Gibson seemed to fit the bill. There has been discussion over the years about whether Winston Churchill or Anthony Eden may have had a hand in this issue, as the premier clearly liked the young officer, who had shown an ability to make speeches and pull-in the crowds.

Gibson, somewhat surprisingly, appears to have been interested in becoming a Member of Parliament, as soon as Garfield Weston approached him. Whether this was because Gibson believed his operational flying days were numbered is unclear, but it may also indicate that he thought he was not destined for a higher rank in the Royal Air Force. Why he might believe this is unknown, but for a Wing Commander and at the time, the most highly decorated officer in the RAF to be even considering politics, does pose some questions.

Guy discussed the matter with Eve and the two went to stay with Garfield Weston and his family at their home in Buckinghamshire over the weekend of 5-6 February. Eve probably thought this was the best way to divert her husband away from operations and into a safer vocation. Eventually, Guy agreed to be considered by the local Conservative Party and would be vetted by the local chairman.

Garfield Weston knew his replacement needed to attend the constituency to get to know the chairman and various other influential figures. He knew the experienced diplomat

Lord Vansittart, was due to visit the constituency after the weekend, so he arranged for Guy and Eve to attend a party at the Macclesfield Arms Hotel on 9 February 1944.

In between visiting the Weston family home and Macclesfield, Guy still managed to fit in a visit to the American B-17 base at RAF Kimbolton in north Cambridgeshire, on Monday, 7 February. Once again, the media were on hand to photograph him meeting the two pilots of one bomber called 'Dragon Lady.'

After a lengthy selection process which included a number of other potential candidates, including Air Vice-Marshal Don Bennett, commander of the Pathfinder Force and a man who would feature later in Gibson's life; Guy was eventually selected to be the Conservative Party's prospective parliamentary candidate for Macclesfield at the next general election. On face value, it appeared it would only be a matter of time before Guy Gibson left the RAF behind and entered the world of politics and Westminster.

Most people often consider senior military officers to be more like politicians than service personnel, so the question is whether both Guy Gibson and his seniors believed he had the character and competencies to become a senior staff officer? If they did, why allow him to go off to become an MP and not become a staff officer? Maybe they thought he might be more useful in a post war government, but maybe they knew his character was more bombastic than diplomatic.

On the night of 12-13 February 1944, Gibson lost another close associate from No. 617 Squadron when Flight Lieutenant Bob Hay, his old bombing leader, was killed. Hay was flying with Harold 'Mick' Martin and bombing the Anthéor Viaduct when their Lancaster was hit by flak and he was killed. When Gibson received this news is unknown.

Guy Gibson remained a public figure and continued to attend various public meetings, giving morale boosting speeches, but some appointments were very different.

On 19 February, Guy appeared on the popular BBC radio program *Desert Island Discs* with its presenter Roy Plomley. The two men discussed service life and Guy chose the requisite number of records, giving a reason for each of the tracks he selected.

The Royal Air Force March Past was a track Gibson was very familiar with and he told Roy Plomley, 'It always sent a shiver down his spine.' Another favourite he introduced was the *US Marines Hymn*, otherwise known as the *Shores of Tripoli.* He explained that his affection for this march, stemmed from hearing it during his recent visit to the United States of America. Other tracks reminded him of his wife, but more surprisingly, he included two tracks by Adolf Hitler's favourite composer – Richard Wagner. He selected the *Flying Dutchman* for its links to his favourite pastime of sailing and the *Ride of the Valkyries*, the tempo of which he said, reminded him of a bombing raid.

The Warsaw Concerto by Richard Addinsell was another piece which reminded him of the Officers' Mess, recalling this would be played over and over again in the Mess. Gibson also enjoyed the *'A thousand and one nights'* waltz by Johann Strauss II. As well as the marches and classical music, he also selected Bing Crosby's song *'If I had my way'*.

The fact Guy had taken part in *Desert Island Discs* must have made him realise his operational flying days had gone.

The German listening services would have been recording this broadcast, storing it away like any intelligence service to use at a later date if Gibson ever fell into their hands. Surely, he knew he was now permanently grounded?

As already mentioned, in mid-February the fifth member of his dams crew - Flight Sergeant John Pulford, was killed when his Lancaster flew into a hill in West Sussex due to poor visibility. A few weeks later, on the night of 31 March, the final member of his crew, rear gunner Richard Trevor-Roper, was shot down and killed on board a No. 97 Squadron Lancaster by German ace Major Drewes of III/NJG1.

Further public appearances continued and Guy visited the Colston Hall in Bristol, to support the blood transfusion service and to appeal for more donations. He could not escape giving a blood donation of his own, before taking the obligatory cup of tea and signing autographs for the Red Cross nurses and the adoring public. Not surprisingly, the media were quick to photograph the returning Dams hero giving his blood and signing autographs. What some of them ignored or rather the censor deleted, was a thinly veiled attack on the RAF and Air Marshal Harris's strategic bombing campaign against Germany. Similar in many ways to his speech in Canada some months before, he was meant to extol the virtues and necessities of blood donations to the war effort, but Gibson sidetracked into stating that people should rid themselves of the belief, that bombing alone could win the war. He was clearly unhappy with the Commander-in-Chief's policy and probably the increasing number of his friends who were being killed carrying out this continuous assault.

Gibson was probably only echoing the thoughts of most bomber crews who at that time were engaged on the Battle of Berlin and the massed attacks aimed at the German capital. Losses were high and many believed there was no sign of the German war machine cracking.

In mid-March 1944, despite his pending candidacy for Macclesfield, Gibson was sent on a staff officers course at the RAF Staff College, Bulstrode Park, Gerrards Cross, to the north-west of London. So perhaps there were some who believed he was higher command material?

While he was at the Staff College, learning the finer details of senior command, Gibson continued to work on his book *Enemy Coast Ahead*. He was still married to Eve, but he remained in contact with Margaret and he soon took advantage of his current posting to visit her at her home on the South Coast.

In May 1944, Guy and Margaret met one last time in Bognor Regis, it being a relatively short journey of less than sixty miles from the Staff College.

Guy was no longer in command of a squadron and officially he was off operations, but he was still deeply enamoured with Margaret, even though she was now married. In the *Daily Mail* newspaper in October 2010, Margaret claimed that during this final meeting, Guy promised to return for her after the war was over. It was the last time the two would meet. (There is possible confusion over whether this was the correct date for this final meeting. In his book *Guy Gibson*, Professor Richard Morris states their last meeting was in July 1944, having interviewed Margaret himself in the early 1990s.)

On the first anniversary of the Dams raid, there was a dance at the Petwood Hotel in Woodhall Spa, Lincolnshire, now home to No. 617 Squadron. The hotel was the Officers' Mess and the squadron was still commanded by Wing Commander Leonard Cheshire. Gibson was unable to attend the anniversary event, but he did manage to attend as the honoured guest at another dance a few days later on 20 May. Gibson standing on a table, made a speech alongside Cheshire, the current commander of his old squadron.

Gibson must have stood wondering about *his* squadron with so many of those he knew having been killed or posted missing in action. Against the odds, Gibson had built the unit from scratch and performed the most famous raid in history, but now he was just a mere passing celebrity guest.

Leonard Cheshire was a very different person to Guy Gibson. He was much more reserved, studious and less of a party animal. Unlike Gibson he was happy to converse with the lower ranks and ground crews, something which endeared him to them. However, when he first arrived to take command, this change of character was not liked by the squadron's aircrews – especially as they had not seen many operations since the Dams raid. Whereas Gibson was writing *Enemy Coast Ahead,* Cheshire had already published a book titled *Bomber Pilot* in early 1943 and this did not initially endear him to some of the squadron. In time, Cheshire would gain the respect of the aircrews and prove himself to be worthy of the Victoria Cross.

The relationship between Guy Gibson and Leonard Cheshire is an issue that is often missed or ignored by historians. Although the two men had very little contact, it appears

Cheshire was someone who possibly irritated Gibson, or rather his command of the Dambuster squadron did, as did his close relationship with Air Vice-Marshal Cochrane, the AOC of No. 5 Group. When he was awarded the Victoria Cross, Cheshire, who already had the DSO and two bars plus a DFC, overtook Gibson to become the most highly decorated man in the Royal Air Force. Could Guy Gibson have been jealous?

Leonard Cheshire had taken command of Gibson's No. 617 Squadron in late 1943, taking over from the temporary commander Harold 'Mick' Martin, a man who had been part of the Dams raid. Leonard Cheshire would later recall, that he learnt all he could about low-level flying from Martin (as Gibson had before the Dams raid) and this was put to good effect when they started to develop a procedure for low-level target marking. As we shall see in a later chapter, in February 1944, these new low-level tactics were sold to the Commander-in-Chief of Bomber Command – Arthur Harris – by Ralph Cochrane.

Gibson completed his staff officers course towards the end of the month of May and his mind started to wander once again. He was still the prospective Conservative parliamentary candidate for Macclesfield, but his mind, as always, continually returned to the thought of flying and more particularly, operational flying.

Guy managed to obtain another period of leave and he went with Eve to North Wales. Once again, he was in a small dinghy sailing it around the bay, often in poor weather, while Eve stayed on shore and under shelter. Apart from flying, sailing was still Gibson's favourite pastime, but his marriage was in the doldrums and it was becoming something of a charade. Whether Eve ever knew of his contact with Margaret is not known.

According to Richard Morris in his book *Guy Gibson,* there was by this time, rumours that Gibson, 'Spent more time in bed with other chaps' wives than he ever did in the air.' Morris does not give any evidence to support these allegations and I have been unable to find any myself, but it appears from the comment about his behaviour in Canada and his relationship with Margaret, that there could have been some infidelity by Gibson. He was clearly something of a ladies man, while being deeply and affectionately involved with Margaret, although there was never any admission that this was anything other than a platonic relationship. At the same time, he was friendly, but maybe nothing more than that, with a number of other females he knew and worked with.

While Guy and Eve were in North Wales in early June 1944, the invasion of Normandy was announced. Gibson was excited by the news and desperate to return to action, but Eve managed to make him stay on leave for another couple of days. Despite her pleas, he contacted Air Marshal Arthur Harris begging to be returned to the front line. Whatever was said between the two is unclear, but four days later, on 12 June 1944, Wing Commander Guy Gibson was posted to the Staff of No. 55 Base at East Kirkby in Lincolnshire.

No. 55 Base managed a number of bomber squadrons based at East Kirkby and Spilsby, as well as for administrative reasons, an adjoining Coastal Command base at Strubby. The three bomber units, Nos. 630, 57 and 207 Squadrons came under the remit of No. 55 Base and in essence, Gibson was now close to three operational units once again, although in a non-flying role. The base and his new role also fell under the control of his former boss, Air Vice-Marshal Ralph Cochrane, the Air Officer Commanding No. 5 Group.

Guy Gibson had completed the manuscript of his book which would eventually become *Enemy Coast Ahead.* On 1 August 1944, he wrote to his London-based publishers Pearn, Pollinger and Higham, stating, 'I cannot seem to think of a good title for this book, but on a separate bit of paper enclosed I have put down a few suggestions.' Gibson gave the following suggestions: Four Years Lifetime, Flak-Fun-Fear, The Boys Die Young, Enemy Coast Ahead, Eight Are Missing, Reich Wreckers and By Fire and By Water.

According to an article in the *Daily Mail* on 13 June 2013, the publishers eventually chose the title *Enemy Coast Ahead* and the book was finally published, posthumously, in 1946.

Guy Gibson's letter to the publishers was sold at auction for £6,600 to a Second World War enthusiast from Europe, but it gives an excellent insight into the man's thought processes and experiences.

At East Kirkby, Gibson soon came across an old acquaintance from No. 106 Squadron in the form of Ron Williams, who was now with No. 57 Squadron. Williams was now a Flight Lieutenant and navigator to Squadron Leader Wyness, the 'B' Flight Commander. In a letter to his parents on 21 June 1944 and now held in the Imperial War Museum, Ron Williams was clearly less than impressed to meet Gibson again:

> 'I forgot to tell you last letter, that my old friend Wing Commander Gibson has been posted to this station (not on flying duties). He recognised me from former times and had a few words to say – I still don't think much of him.'

After just two weeks at East Kirkby, Gibson managed to get behind the controls of an Airspeed Oxford on 28 June and flew himself and Flight Lieutenant Walters to the No. 207 Squadron base at Spilsby. A few days later, in early July, probably to the disgust of Ron Williams, Gibson went up with Squadron Leader Wyness and his crew in a 57 Squadron Lancaster from East Kirkby. The flight was just a local air test, but it only served to rekindle Guy Gibson's enthusiasm for operational flying.

Ron Williams, in another letter home to his parents on 4 July, had to begrudgingly acknowledge that Gibson had flown the aircraft stating, 'He did the flying, the first time in a Lanc for eight months. He coped quite well.'

What is interesting is that Williams's letter to his parents was dated 4 July, but Gibson's flying-logbook gives the date of the flight as 5 July. This therefore appears to have been evidence that Gibson did not keep his logbook up to date like many other airmen.

On 10 July 1944, Gibson was visited by another one of his former No. 617 Squadron officers, this time it was Squadron Leader Harold 'Mick' Martin who flew in from Little Straughton in a de Havilland Mosquito. Martin took Gibson for a *spin* in the agile twin engine night-fighter and he was reportedly amazed by its speed and manoeuvrability. In his flying logbook, Gibson noted both Martin and himself as the pilot.

Harold 'Mick' Martin, having left No. 617 Squadron, was supposedly 'off' operations at the time and part of the staff at No. 151 Squadron, however he still managed to get in a few trips across Europe – something which must have stirred the operational ambitions of Gibson. Once back on the ground, the two men reportedly talked at length. In his book, Richard Morris states that Martin told him personally some years later, that Gibson confided in him that he had doubts about his own political candidature in Macclesfield. Martin was also clear that Gibson was by that time, desperate to return to front-line operational flying.

In July 1944, No. 617 Squadron's commander Leonard Cheshire was awarded the Victoria Cross after completing four operational tours on bombers. He was not recognised for a single event like Guy Gibson, but for his outstanding service over the four tours of operations, which included his work developing low-level target marking. The official announcement was not made until 5 September 1944, but on 8 July, Ralph Cochrane removed Cheshire from operations together with three surviving Dambusters: Les Munro, Dave Shannon and Joe McCarthy. Cheshire's last operational flight was on the night of 7-8 July 1944, when he flew as a low-level target marker in a P-51 Mustang.

Whether Guy Gibson had heard of Cheshire's VC in July is unknown, but he was certainly aware of his low-level target marking operations in 1944. It is said Gibson was less than happy with Leonard Cheshire's Victoria Cross, a possible indication of his resentment of the fact Cheshire had taken command of *his* 617 Squadron and had helped devise low-level target marking, while becoming something of a favourite with Air Vice-Marshal Ralph Cochrane.

What is unclear, is whether 'Mick' Martin, when he met Gibson in early July, unintentionally riled his old commander with accounts of Cheshire's accomplishments and the pending VC? Could it be, Cheshire, who was now being seen as the new hero of Bomber Command, had further frustrated Gibson and added impetus to his desire to return to operations?

On 19 July, Gibson managed to get himself aboard a No. 630 Squadron Lancaster (coded LE-N) at East Kirkby and set off to attack the V1 flying bomb sites and storage areas around Creil near Paris. Gibson, in his flying logbook, stated that he was the pilot and the second pilot and/or passenger was Squadron Leader Miller. The crew were not named. Gibson also added that there was moderate flak and a 'successful aiming point' at the target.

The Master Bomber that day, or as No. 5 Group called the role – the Controller – was Squadron Leader Charles Owen, a man who a few weeks later, would be one of the last people to speak with Gibson before his death. He had just become a controller, having previously flown Lancasters with No. 97 Squadron and he knew Guy Gibson well.

According to the No. 630 Squadron Operational Record Book (ORB), the only Squadron Leader Miller flying that day, was a navigator aboard aircraft serial number PB244 which took off at 19:24hrs and returned home at 23:20hrs. No identification letter for the aircraft was given in the ORB. The pilot was listed as Flight Sergeant Bowers, the flight engineer Sergeant G. Stott, the bomb aimer Sergeant McLaughlan and the wireless operator Sergeant Thompson. The mid-upper gunner was Sergeant Langridge and the rear gunner Warrant Officer Carrier. There is no mention in the operations record book of Wing Commander Guy Gibson being on board this or any other aircraft that day. However, the aircraft (PB244) with a different crew were shot down on 18 August 1944, with the aircraft shown in other records being coded LE-N.

It is therefore clear, Guy Gibson took the controls on 19 July of Lancaster PB244 (coded LE-N) from Flight Sergeant Bowers, while naming Miller as the other pilot/passenger, possibly because he did not want to admit he was flying with an NCO pilot.

Although his flight may have been tacitly authorised by a senior officer, there is no doubt Guy Gibson knew very well, he was prohibited from operations and so too did the officer responsible for completing the ORB entry that day. However, just like in his youth, Gibson was apparently happy to disobey orders, something that could be considered hypocritical for such a commanding disciplinarian.

In the International Bomber Command Centre's digital archive, there is an audio statement from Sergeant (later Warrant Officer) Harry Parkins, who flew as a flight engineer with No. 630 Squadron at this time. In his lengthy statement he says:

> 'I had a mate, a flight engineer, who used to go on the same sort of ops... we got very friendly and if we managed to get back, we'd go into the pub and exchange

> stories, and this particular time he was right down in the mouth, he wouldn't have a drink and I couldn't get him to talk… I kept talking to him and in the end, he said, "I've been sworn not to say anything." Eventually I got him to talk…he said, "Alright then, you know we're the last ones to get in the plane after our inspection? I was just going up the ladder and this bloke come up to me, pushed me out the way and before I knew it, he was on the plane. I didn't know what to do, so I pulled the ladder up and went up to my position and when I got there, this bloke was sat in my seat and he just said 'bugger off down the back' and I was just about to shout at him when the pilot said 'ssh, it's Guy Gibson', so I shut up…all the way over he was criticising everybody, the gunners, the navigator wasn't doing it right, the pilot wasn't watching this and watching that."'

Harry's friend added that when they got to the target, they went round and dropped their bombs, 'The idea was you normally got away quickly, but Gibson said, "Hang on, go round I want to have a look" and he made the pilot go round about three times before they flew off and all the way back, he still criticised them all. Just as they were coming into land, Gibson said, "I want to speak to every member of the crew, I want you to swear an oath that you never saw me in this plane."'

Gibson is said to have brought back a photograph of the aiming point for the target at Creil and a copy was included in his flying logbook, was this the reason they went round so many

Gibson and his No. 106 Squadron flight commanders Searby and Ward-Hunt at Coningsby circa October 1942-May 1943. (IWM)

Debriefing after the Dams raid. Standing: AM Harris & AVM Cochrane. Seated facing L-R: Sqn Ldr Townson intel officer, Spafford and Taerum. R-L front: Trevor-Roper, Hutchison, Gibson and Deering. (IWM)

Gibson with his Liverpudlian radio operator on No. 106 Squadron and No. 617 Squadron – Flight Lieutenant Robert Hutchison DFC circa 1942-1943. His liberated Luftwaffe life jacket, worn from 1941 to the Dams raid and perhaps until his death, can clearly be seen in this image. (© Crown/MoD Copyright, 2024)

Surviving aircraft captains/pilots from the Dams raid, outside the Officers' Mess, taken 17 May 1943. Note Sergeants Townsend and Anderson are on the left, apparently detached from the officers – clearly Anderson had yet to be told of his dismissal from No. 617 Squadron. (IWM)

Above left, above right and below: Three different official portraits of Guy Gibson. While they portray his youthful looks, the image on the left is the stern face many of those who crossed him may remember. The lower image clearly displays his Luftwaffe life jacket. (All © Crown/MoD Copyright, 2024)

Gibson in a classic media portrait believed post Dams raid. (© Crown/MoD Copyright, 2024)

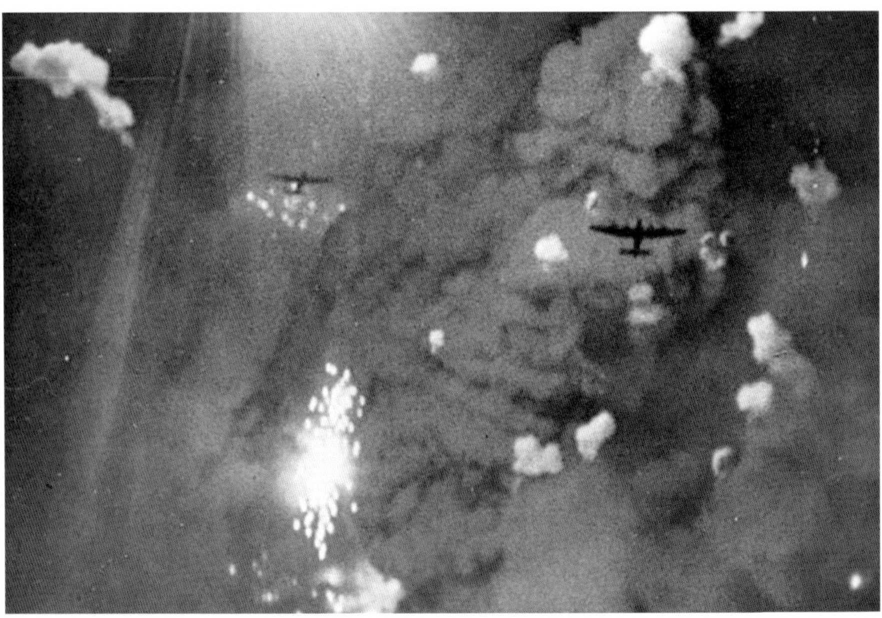

TI's and flak surround bombers, the TI is in the lower left, the various white spots being the burning candles. (IWM)

Gibson meeting Sir Archibald Sinclair and Air Commodore Sharp on 9 September 1944 – ten days before Gibson's final flight. This may have been the last image taken of Gibson. (IWM)

Wing Commander Charles Owen photographed sometime after Gibson's death. (Courtesy of Oliver Owen)

Steenbergen taken about 1940-1941. The crash site is upper left in the light coloured open land, the Van der Riet farm is just above it alongside the small road. The sugar factory is below it near the town centre. The large church can be seen in the town centre, the main road Blauwstraat is running from the south towards the church. Gibson and Warwick were buried in the cemetery to the south end of the road in this image. (No known copyright public domain)

A piece of the de Havilland Mosquito KB267, recovered in 1985 and presented to the RAF Staff College at Bracknell. (M. Mace)

Above and below: A de Havilland Mosquito similar to that flown by Gibson on the 19 September 1944 and a demonstration 1,000lb target indicator with the case removed showing green candles. (Author)

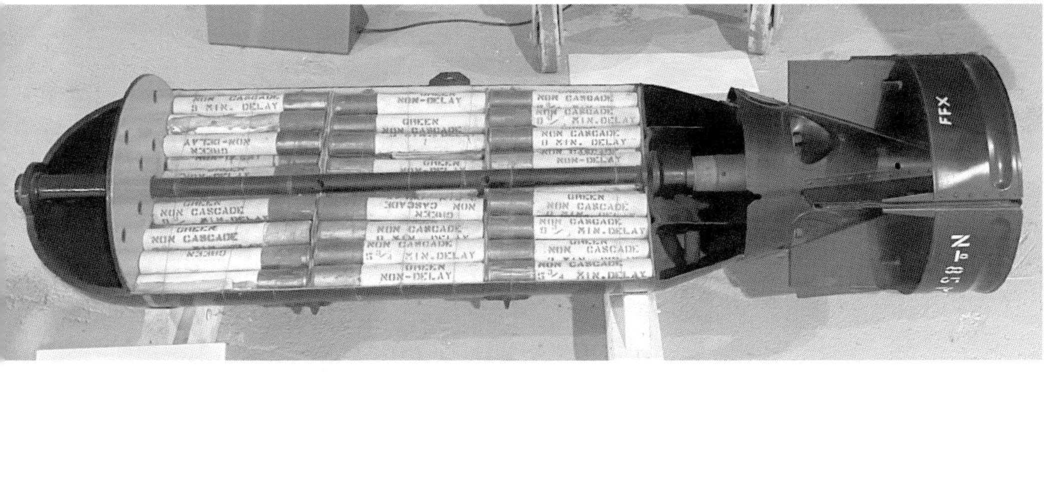

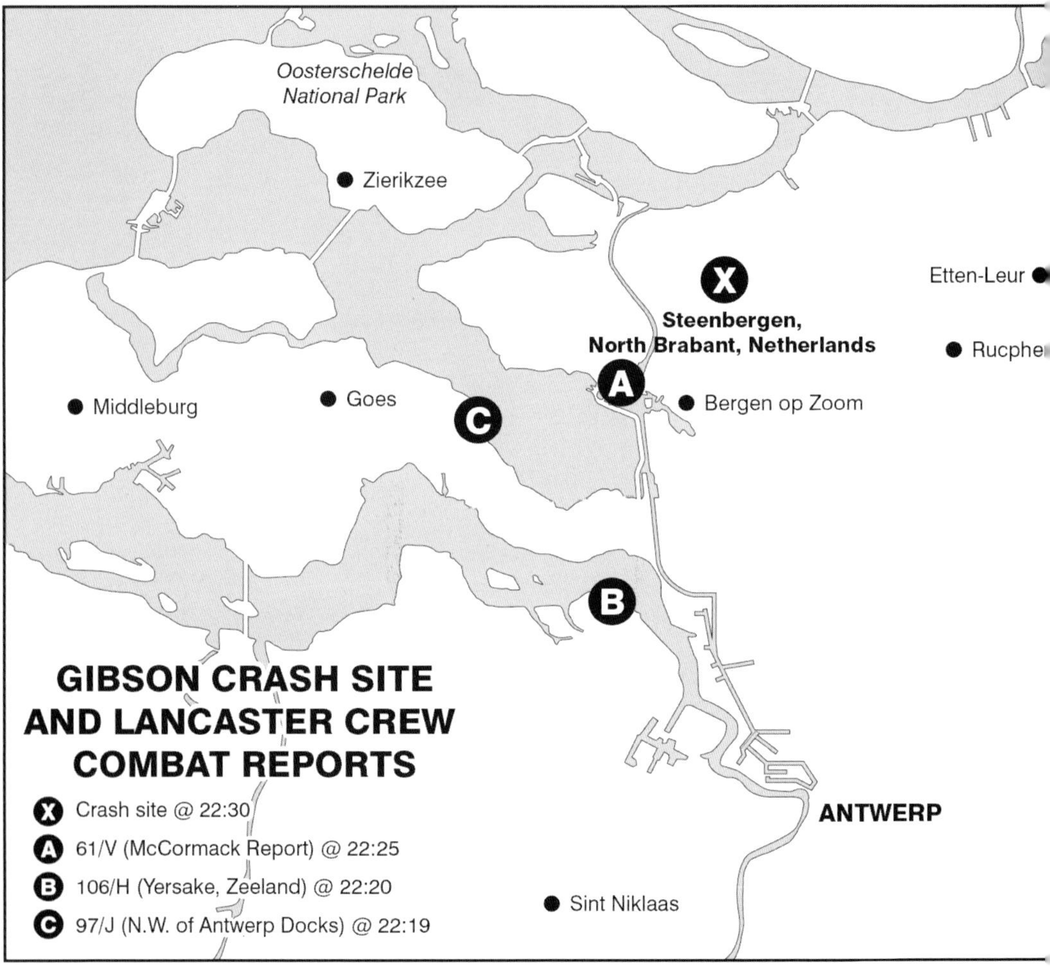
Oosterschelde
National Park
Zierikzee
Etten-Leur
Steenbergen,
North Brabant, Netherlands
Middleburg
Goes
Bergen op Zoom
ANTWERP
Sint Niklaas
GIBSON CRASH SITE
AND LANCASTER CREW
COMBAT REPORTS
X Crash site @ 22:30
A 61/V (McCormack Report) @ 22:25
B 106/H (Yersake, Zeeland) @ 22:20
C 97/J (N.W. of Antwerp Docks) @ 22:19

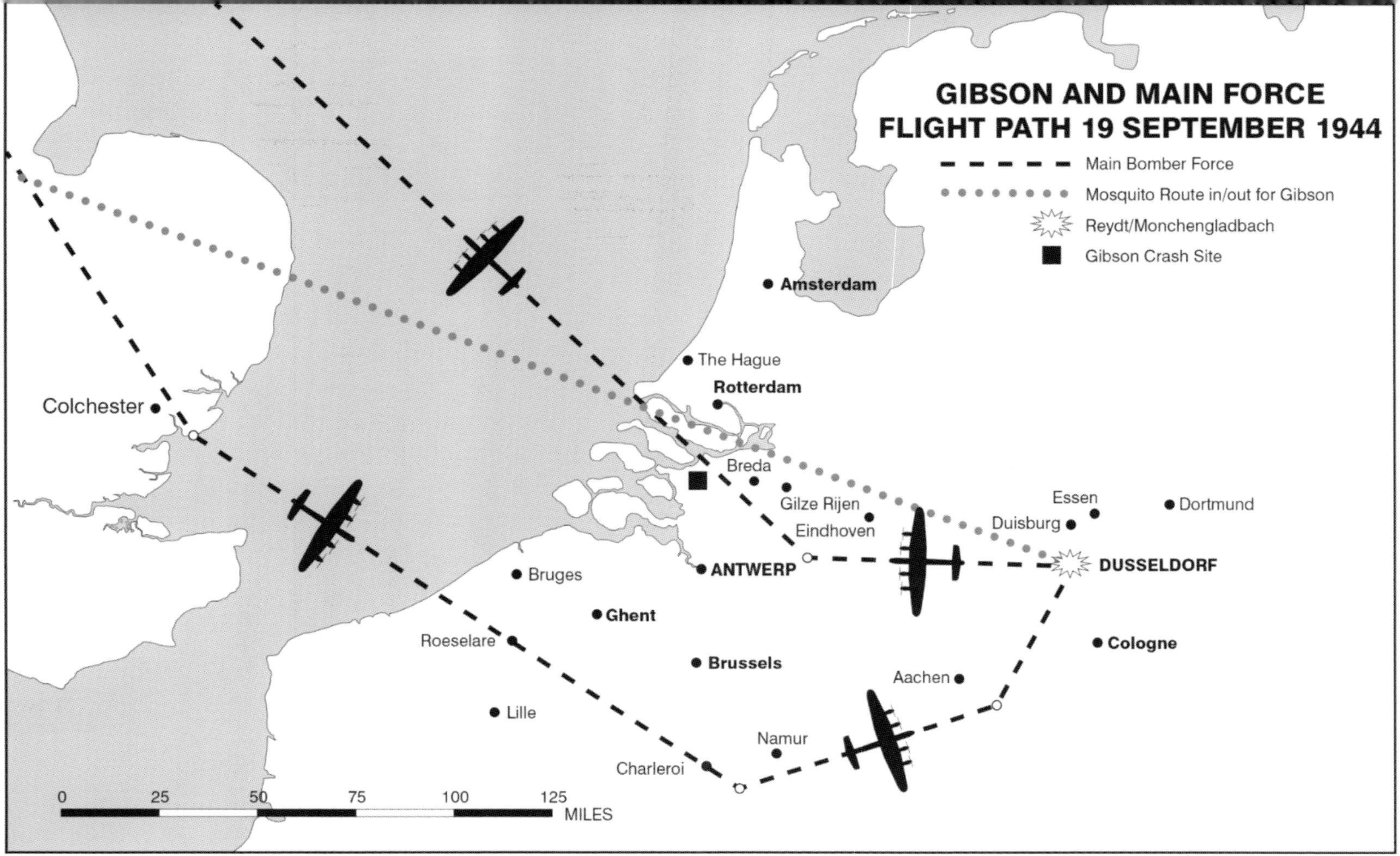
GIBSON AND MAIN FORCE
FLIGHT PATH 19 SEPTEMBER 1944
Main Bomber Force
Mosquito Route in/out for Gibson
Reydt/Monchengladbach
Gibson Crash Site
Amsterdam
The Hague
Rotterdam
Colchester
Breda
Gilze Rijen
Eindhoven
Essen
Dortmund
Duisburg
DUSSELDORF
ANTWERP
Bruges
Ghent
Roeselare
Brussels
Cologne
Aachen
Lille
Namur
Charleroi
0
25
50
75
100
125
MILES

The graves of Gibson and his navigator James Warwick in Steenbergen cemetery. (M. Mace)

The streets on the industrial site which now covers the crash site bear the names Gibsonstraat, Warwickstraat and Mosquitostraat in memory of their loss. (M. Mace)

Warwickstraat
James Warwick, squadron leader R.A.F.,
met G. Gibson bij deze straat neergestort
en omgekomen 19-9-1944

Mosquitostraat
Warwickstraat

The people of Steenbergen have done a lot to remember Gibson and Warwick, but it is difficult to make an old crash site in an industrial site look appropriate. The wooden post on which a plaque is placed may have some significance and may have been found at the crash site, but this is unclear. (All site images courtesy of M. Mace)

MOSQUITO KB 267 CRASHED HERE 19 SEPTEMBER 1944
CAPTAIN– WING COMMANDER G P GIBSON VC DSO DFC. WHO LED THE DAMBUSTERS RAID ON 16/17 MAY 1943.
NAVIGATOR– SQUADRON LEADER J B WARWICK DFC.
BOTH OFFICERS LOST THEIR LIVES IN THE SERVICE OF THEIR COUNTRY.
"OH I HAVE SLIPPED THE SURLY BONDS OF EARTH REACHED OUT AND TOUCHED THE FACE OF GOD"
DEEP RESPECT

MOSQUITO KB 267 CRASHED HERE 19 SEPTEMBER 1944
CAPTAIN- WING COMMANDER G P GIBSON VC DSO DFC. WHO LED THE DAMBUSTERS RAID ON 16/17 MAY 1943.
NAVIGATOR- SQUADRON LEADER J B WARWICK DFC.
BOTH OFFICERS LOST THEIR LIVES IN THE SERVICE OF THEIR COUNTRY.
"OH I HAVE SLIPPED THE SURLY BONDS OF EARTH REACHED OUT AND TOUCHED THE FACE OF GOD"

A more suitable memorial to Gibson and Warwick was placed by the local population in Zuidwal park, in the centre of the town. The propellor is not from the Mosquito which was virtually obliterated in the crash, but is said to be from a Lancaster wreck. (M. Mace)

TER NAGEDACHTENIS AAN
W/CDR GUY GIBSON VC DSO DFC
SQN/LDR JIM WARWICK DFC
ROYAL AIR FORCE
BEIDEN VERLOREN HUN LEVEN TE
STEENBERGEN 19 SEPTEMBER 1944
FOR OUR TOMORROW
THEY GAVE THEIR TODAY
LEST WE FORGET
OP VLEUGELS VAN VRIJHEID
VOCHTEN EN VIELEN ZIJ
IN DE HARTEN VAN MENSEN
VAN NU EN VAN MORGEN
LEVEN ZIJ VOORT

times and was Harry's friend Flight Engineer G. Stott on the aircraft PB244 (LE-N) on 19 July?

If this story is correct and corroborates the other information, clearly Guy Gibson knew he was breaking the rules and was even happy to stow away, just to go on an operational flight. His name does not appear in the squadron's Operations Record Book, but it appears he was happy to list it in his own flying logbook, with the navigator, Squadron Leader Miller, as the pilot or passenger rather than Flight Sergeant Bowers. It would also appear his subterfuge was aided and abetted by No. 630 Squadron's ORB's author.

Coming just over a week after he confided his concerns to 'Mick' Martin, it is clear, with the benefit of hindsight, that Gibson was on the proverbial edge and desperate to return to operations. The Allied armies were advancing across Belgium and France and Gibson was surrounded by front-line squadrons and their crews. It was probably too much for him to bear and he needed to be part of the final bombing campaign against Nazi Germany.

On 26 July, Gibson flew a Lancaster on another trial flight, but it was not enough for him. What was being said behind closed doors or down the various telephone lines is unknown, but it must be assumed he was still pleading with Cochrane and Harris to be allowed to return to front-line operations.

In his book *Strike Hard, Strike Sure,* Ralph Barker claims on page 114-5 of the 1965 edition, that Guy Gibson had been found in his office, 'With tears in his eyes, heartbroken at being separated from his beloved crews.' Barker adds that this information got back to Air Vice-Marshal Cochrane and Air Marshal Harris, who quickly relented and posted Gibson to RAF Coningsby. The source of this information was Harris himself. In his foreword to *Enemy Coast Ahead*, Harris states:

> 'In a third and final effort to force him to rest from operations, he (Gibson) was put on his Group's staff. A few days later he was found in his office with – literally – tears in his eyes at being separated from his beloved crews and unable to go on operations.'

Harris's foreword continued with another admission:

> 'He always had direct access to me, and on further pressure from him and his AOC, I quite wrongly allowed him to return to operations.'

Air Marshal Harris clearly blamed himself for Guy Gibson's death, but he appears to have also been laying some of the blame at the feet of Ralph Cochrane the AOC of No. 5 Group.

In many ways, Guy Gibson had laid the foundations for his return to operations and ultimately his own death. However, he was *just* a Wing Commander, all be it one with a Victoria Cross and a host of other decorations. Could an Air Marshal, the Commander-in-Chief of Bomber Command and an Air Vice-Marshal have not ordered him to stay away from operations and remain grounded? Or was the aurora that still surrounded the Dambuster Guy Gibson so strong, they had to give in to him?

Whatever pleading and bargaining was taking place, unrecorded behind the scenes, Gibson was quickly posted to No. 54 Base Headquarters at Coningsby on 2 August 1944.

Gibson arrived at his old station two days later and whether by design or it was just a coincidence, the No. 5 Group Air Officer Commanding, Air Vice-Marshal Ralph Cochrane was also visiting the base and spoke with him. What was discussed and what Gibson was told he could and could not do is not recorded, but within seven weeks Guy Gibson would be dead.

Chapter Six

Non-operational

Guy Gibson had quickly transferred and started work as the Base Air Staff Officer (BASO) at Coningsby in Lincolnshire. His new home provided target marking and illumination for raids by the bomber squadrons of No. 5 Group.

The airfield was home to the Lancaster equipped Nos. 83 and 97 Squadrons, who provided illumination with flares to allow low-flying target markers to identify aiming points for the main bomber force. The two squadrons at Coningsby had originally been part of No. 5 Group, before they were sent to join the new No. 8 Group Pathfinder Force in 1942. In 1944, they were returned to No. 5 Group to assist Air Vice-Marshal Ralph Cochrane to develop his new concept of low-level target marking.

Based at nearby Woodhall Spa was Gibson's old unit, No. 617 Squadron, and a dedicated low-level target marking unit which was equipped with de Havilland Mosquitos – No. 627 Squadron. Various other squadrons of Lancasters from No. 5 Group operated from a variety of airfields around the county, as well as just over the border in Nottinghamshire, while their Group headquarters was based in Grantham.

No. 5 Group was seen by some as the most elite unit within Bomber Command. However, the Group and the personalities at the head of it, were believed by some to have been divisive and Air Vice-Marshal Donald Bennett, the head of No. 8 Pathfinder Group certainly thought so.

Donald Bennett is one of the most interesting characters linked to the story of Guy Gibson. He was the first commander of the dedicated Pathfinder Force created in July 1942 and an expert long-range pilot. He developed the Pathfinder Force (PFF) making him the top expert on target marking and Pathfinders, but his Pathfinder force utilised a very different system to that of Cochrane's No. 5 Group – the type of low-level marking operation on which Guy Gibson would lose his life, just a few weeks after his arrival at Coningsby.

As we have already seen, Donald Bennett stood unsuccessfully as a candidate against Guy Gibson for selection as the prospective parliamentary candidate for Macclesfield. He was eventually elected at a bye-election as the Member of Parliament for Middlesborough West in 1945, but lost his seat after less than three months at the 1945 General Election. Various further attempts to be re-elected to parliament failed, the last being in the 1974 General Election.

Donald Bennett had been a pre-war pilot and commanded Nos. 10 and 77 Bomber Squadrons in 1941-42. In mid-1942, he was shot down on a raid to sink the battleship *Tirpitz* in a Norwegian fjord. He managed to escape via neutral Sweden and returned to Britain, being awarded the Distinguished Service Order in June 1942. The following month he became the head of the newly established No. 8 Group Pathfinder Force.

In 1943, with the success of the Pathfinder Force (PFF), he was promoted first to Air Commodore and eventually to Air

Vice-Marshal. Although Air Marshal Arthur Harris initially dismissed the idea of a Pathfinder force, thinking it would lead to an elite group which would undermine the sterling efforts and morale of all his bomber squadrons, he eventually agreed to the venture.

In his autobiography *Pathfinder* published in 1958, Donald Bennett fails to hide his apparent anger with No. 5 Group, or more particularly, their AOC Ralph Cochrane. Bennett states in the book that No. 5 Group was the strongest in the command at the time (1942), its Air Officer Commanding being Alec Coryton, while Ralph Cochrane was AOC of No. 3 Group.

Donald Bennett recounts that Harris, who was by this time Commander-in-Chief of Bomber Command, ordered Coryton and Cochrane to send twelve Lancasters from each Group to bomb Berlin; the thinking being such a small formation might slip through the considerable German defences. Coryton told Harris it was too risky a venture and he would not send his crews, but Cochrane, being a new AOC and an old squadron associate of Harris, agreed to do this.

Bennett states that for this and for 'other reasons' which he did not specify, Coryton was relieved of his command of the elite No. 5 Group, which was immediately given to Ralph Cochrane. Bennett says on page 168 of his book, that he had nothing personally against Ralph Cochrane, but, 'As an Air Force officer, I found him most unfortunate.'

This comment appears primarily aimed at Ralph Cochrane, but Bennett was being a little disingenuous, as he previously had issues with Coryton over his new Pathfinding Force. This was evident on 28 November 1942, three months after the start of No. 8 Group's PFF operations, when the various Bomber Group AOCs met at RAF Wyton to discuss the use and tactics of the new Pathfinders. While the AOCs of the other groups were happy, Alec Coryton from No. 5 Group wanted more ground marking and less illumination by flares. So perhaps Bennett had an issue with No. 5 Group rather than the two men who held the post of Air Officer Commanding?

Guy Gibson's No. 617 Squadron were members of No. 5 Group and Don Bennett did not take kindly to what he deemed as 'headline grabbing expeditions.' His apparent animosity towards Cochrane and No. 5 Group would peak again in April 1944, when Arthur Harris decided to allow the Group to form its own low-level target markers.

In early 1944, towards the end of Bomber Command's four-month campaign against Berlin, Air Vice-Marshal Ralph Cochrane approached Harris and suggested the best way to mark a target was from just fifty feet above the roof tops with de Havilland Mosquitos. Harris immediately contacted Donald Bennett by telephone to discuss Cochrane's idea, but it was instantly dismissed by the Pathfinder Force commander, who stated it was too difficult and the target indicators (TIs) could not be seen under a cloud layer by a bomber force at a higher altitude. Within half an hour of the telephone calls termination, Donald Bennett, in his book, says he was told to report to Bomber Command HQ.

Once he arrived at Bomber Command HQ, Bennett was told to immediately release Nos. 83 and 97 Squadrons from his No. 8 Group Pathfinder Force and send them back to join Cochrane's No. 5 Group. In addition, a Mosquito unit (No. 627

Squadron) was to be sent from No. 8 Group to join Cochrane's new target marking section. Donald Bennett was told the three squadrons would be used by No. 5 Group to undertake their new low-level method of target marking.

Bennett took this very personally, believing it to be a 'slap in the face' for the men of his dedicated Pathfinder Force. It also led him to believe the Commander-in-Chief of Bomber Command, was displaying a total lack of confidence in No. 8 Group. Bennett did not consider that he had dismissed the low-level marking technique himself and probably laid the foundations for Cochrane's group to specialise in this new type of marking.

Despite his earlier comments, on page 176 of his book *Pathfinder*, Bennett tried to re-emphasise that he had never fallen out with Ralph Cochrane and that those who gossiped and said there was a feud between the two, overlooked the fact they were long-time personal friends. This comment is hard to believe when on the very next page Donald Bennett states, 'Cochrane could do anything and the C-in-C would always support him, any attempts to convince the C-in-C that Cochrane could ever be wrong, were inevitably doomed to failure.'

Donald Bennett continued throughout the book making what some may think were disparaging remarks about Cochrane and No. 5 Group's low-level target marking. Bennett even misspelt Cochrane's name throughout the book, repeatedly missing the letter 'e' off the end of the surname. In fact, Ralph Cochrane was so angered by Bennett's comments in *Pathfinder*, he contacted the publishers requesting changes to the text, which he stated were not only incorrect but libelous.

Considering his comments about Cochrane, it is perhaps surprising, that having failed as a political candidate standing against Gibson in 1944, Donald Bennett never mentions him at all in his book. Guy Gibson was in many ways a favourite of Cochrane and certainly No. 5 Group's 'star' commanding officer. The Dams raid in May 1943 by No. 617 Squadron, again part of No. 5 Group and under Cochrane's command, is not specifically mentioned in the book.

There is however, a perceived *sneer* at the Dams operation on page 185, when Don Bennett states that his own Light Night Striking Force Mosquitos, carried out *other duties* in addition to their regular raids. He specifically notes their raid on the Kiel Canal which caused its closure for two and a half weeks, adding that *his crews* had undertaken just a few hours training before the operation. This he added, was in comparison to 'Some in Bomber Command, who had to go in for intense training for a considerable period, before they undertook any special duty and had to ensure the Public Relations Department were well informed!' Clearly, in the opinion of most people, this was a derogatory statement aimed at Ralph Cochrane, No. 617 Squadron and by extension Guy Gibson.

Although in my opinion, Donald Bennett clearly had issues with Ralph Cochrane, No. 5 Group's low-level target marking, probably the existence of 617 Squadron and the Dams raid itself; I find it curious he does not specifically mention Guy Gibson and his final flight.

Guy Gibson received no known lengthy Pathfinder or target marking training before his fatal flight, when he was operating as Controller of the No. 5 Group low-level target marking force. With Donald Bennett apparently so disgruntled with Cochrane and the No. 5 Group low-level target marking, why did he not question this and Gibson's death? Surely, this was a proverbial open-goal for him. Even if he did not challenge Gibson's personal actions, he could have used it to question the No. 5 Group target marking system and its commander – Ralph Cochrane; but was the issue of Guy Gibson, the nation's hero's death too much and he avoided the matter and further controversy?

Another member of the No. 8 Group Pathfinder hierarchy, was the renowned Group Captain Hamish Mahaddie DSO, DFC, AFC. He flew tours with Bomber Command before becoming an instructor and joining Donald Bennett's staff in March 1943. Hamish Mahaddie went on to become station commander at RAF Warboys, the home of the Pathfinder Training Unit, replacing John Searby, the old No. 106 Squadron acquaintance of Guy Gibson.

After the war Mahaddie wrote his own autobiography: *Hamish* in 1989. In the book, he states that he would visit the various Bomber Group commanders and when he visited No. 5 Group, he would explain the Pathfinders techniques to Ralph 'Cocky' Cochrane.

On one occasion in late 1942 or early 1943, he was talking with Ralph Cochrane when Guy Gibson, the No. 106 Squadron commander was ushered into the office. Cochrane had already given Mahaddie a list of about twenty No. 5 Group pilots he did not want the Pathfinder Force to recruit before Gibson's arrival.

As they left the office together, Mahaddie says Guy Gibson told him bluntly and in no uncertain terms, the fate that awaited him if he was to *steal* one of his crews, adding; 'And keep your sticky fingers off Searby.' Mahaddie later managed to recruit John Searby to the Pathfinders and Gibson's friend probably missed the opportunity to join 617 Squadron and the Dams raid in 1943. Gibson later recovered Dave Shannon from Pathfinder training at Warboys to join his new specialist squadron, something Mahaddie describes in his book as, 'A legitimate reprisal for the Searby snatch.'

It was clear there was a continuous issue between Cochrane and Gibson's No. 5 Group and the Bennett-Mahaddie No. 8 Group Pathfinders.

It was into this political cauldron that Guy Gibson returned in the summer of 1944. He was happy to be back with No. 5 Group and wanted to settle in quickly, hoping to be allowed some operational flying. However, upon arrival, he did not make a good first impression on the Mosquito crews of No. 627 Squadron.

According to Flying Officer Kent Oatley of No. 627 Squadron, in an audio statement held by the International Bomber Command Centre near Lincoln, Guy Gibson did not ingratiate himself with the experienced Mosquito target marker crews at Woodhall Spa.

Ken Oatley met Guy Gibson on several occasions but, not in a personal manner. He recounted:

> 'On one occasion he came into our little bar, we were in Nissen huts that was an airman's hut actually, the whole Mess and the kitchen was all part of it, but we had no bar arrangements, so we had a builder in the squadron

> and he built the bar and a fire in there for us, so we could have an officer's drinking area.
>
> 'One night my pilot, Walker, and three Australians were in there having a drink and the door opened and in walks Gibson. Nobody moved and Gibson said, "Don't you normally stand to attention and when a senior officer comes in?" They looked at each other, said, "No, no, no."
>
> 'Gibson created such a fuss, they grabbed hold of him, took him outside, took his trousers off (de-bagged him) and told him not to come in again. The next morning, there was an officer's parade which Gibson officiated, he went down the line and of course the Australians in their dark uniforms and my pilot, who was a real dure Scotsman, was standing at the end of the line and Gibson put him in the glasshouse for three weeks. Gibson didn't remain very popular with our crowd.'

The same incident was noted by Richard Morris in his biography *Guy Gibson*, but he stated Flight Lieutenant Peter Mallender of No. 627 Squadron had told him in a letter, that Gibson, when he entered the Mess said, 'Don't you know who I am? I am Wing Commander Gibson,' to which one Australian shouted back, 'So bloody what?' The group started chanting 'de-bag, de-bag' and Gibson was seized and de-bagged. The Wing Commander reportedly snapped at one Glaswegian (Walker?), who verbally snapped back at him. For this misdemeanour, according to Mallender, the Scotsman was sent to the Sheffield glasshouse.

Another version of this story appears in the book *Mosquito Men* by David Price, published in 2022. In the book, it is reported that Jock Walker and two Canadians (not Australians) were at the bar when Gibson walked in. What was said, according to Price, is uncertain, but Gibson was unceremoniously bundled outside and de-bagged. Jock Walker was later given fourteen days detention on base by Gibson, but the others escaped punishment as he could not identify them. However, the episode left a bad impression upon the crews of No. 627 Squadron and Guy Gibson was no longer welcome in their Officers' Mess bar.

It appears this story, although there might have been some slight additions or alterations over the years, indicates that Guy Gibson was a little too full of himself, disliked and de-bagged. We have already heard that he liked to be called 'Dambuster', but in the eyes of hardened front-line aircrew, he was just another old retired hero and it was well over a year since the Dams raid. In that time, a lot of other young men had come and gone, many dying on the hundreds of raids since Operation Chastise in May 1943. Guy Gibson's enlarged ego was not welcome and despite his senior rank, it appears the men were even willing to forcibly remove his trousers and throw him out of the Officers' Mess.

The issue of discipline, protocol and King's Regulations is something of a mystery and confused as far as Guy Gibson as a character is concerned. He respected his former commanding officer Charles Widdows for the way in which he handled No. 29 Squadron and he was certainly a disciplinarian himself with 106 and 617 Squadrons; but as we have seen, he could be lax, especially in his younger days before taking command of a squadron.

Perhaps the best example of this 'confused discipline' can be found in Gibson's flying logbook. He did not practice what he preached and did not keep his own running flying hours total up to date. In fact, it appears he also missed some flights completely from his logbook and did not fill in the various columns in detail. For example, rather than entering an aircraft serial number, he would just enter its squadron letter, but that letter could have belonged to various differing machines over a number of months. He did not submit his logbook to his flight commander or station commander for their signature on a regular basis and he certainly made comments in the book, that would make any senior officer smart and reprimand him. His comments about his cannons jamming on his Beaufighter were a perfect example of this. To complete the issue, his spelling and grammar could also be very wayward.

Guy Gibson in a peacetime Royal Air Force may have been an underachiever, a bit like his school days, but in wartime, he was just what the service needed and rather like Douglas Bader (his fellow St. Edwardian at Oxford), he was known to lead from the front and cast the rule book in the waste paper basket whenever he chose. Discipline was important in terms of confronting the enemy and completing the operation, but it appears other aspects could be ignored from time to time.

Gibson desperately wanted to return to front-line operational flying and although there is no evidence to substantiate this theory, the altercation in the 627 Squadron Officers' Mess, may have led in some way to his ultimate demise, by exacerbating his desperation to fly operationally and prove himself once again.

In mid to late August, Gibson decided that politics was not for him and he wrote to the Chair of the Macclesfield Conservative Party resigning his candidature. As the Allied armies pushed the Nazis further back towards the Dutch - German border and the wars conclusion drew nearer, operational flying was all that mattered to Guy Gibson.

Gibson continued to push for a return to front line operations and it is said by some, Ralph Cochrane eventually relented and allowed him to undertake the occasional operational flight, as long as the risk was deemed to be low and his role was non-participatory. This direction that he was to have a non-participatory role is a confusing one. Whether he led the attack, dropped bombs or flew in a Mosquito with a cine camera, it surely did not matter, for he could be shot down and killed in any of these circumstances.

On 10 August, Gibson flew a P-38 Lockheed Lightning around the Lincolnshire countryside. Officially, No. 5 Group had two of these aircraft on loan from the US Army Air Force for evaluation tests and possible alternatives for target marking Mosquitos. However, according to Charles Owen in a letter to the *Aeroplane Monthly* in June 1977, they arrived via Air Commodore Sharp, the Coningsby base commander. After his period as USAAF Liaison Officer where he was very popular, he managed to obtain the loan of a P-47 Thunderbolt, but he did not like it and exchanged it for a P-38 Lightning.

The aircraft had arrived on 20 July 1944 and Charles Owen had flown it on 1, 2, 3 and 6 August before Gibson started to fly the aeroplane. Although he had flown a tour on Bristol Beaufighters, Gibson was a heavy bomber pilot by trade and how he could evaluate the Lightning against the abilities of a Mosquito is unclear; but it appears he was willing to do anything to sharpen his skills as he awaited his anticipated recall to operations. A second similar flight in a P-38 Lightning appears to have been undertaken the following day, once again around the Lincolnshire countryside, but was it enough to satisfy Gibson's appetite for flying?

Oliver Owen, the son of Charles, told the author in early 2024, that the group of pilots at Coningsby which included Gibson, Sharp, Woodroffe, Simpson and Owen, was a highly experienced bunch who in effect had their own collection of aircraft!

On Guy Gibson's twenty-sixth birthday, on 12 August, he met with Eve for lunch in Skegness. At the meal, Guy was said to have been depressed, telling his wife he now wanted a divorce. Eve tried to talk him out of this decision, but he would not accept it. Eventually, after some discussion, he agreed to wait some time, but he seemed adamant that he wanted a divorce.

Gibson was clearly in a major quandary. His marriage was all but finished, it appears he was still besotted with Mary and most of all, he wanted to fly operationally.

It is possible, although apparently not documented, that the two flights on 10-11 August, were not evaluation flights, but preparations for an operational flight on 15 August. That day, Gibson flew one of the P-38 Lockheed Lightnings with Squadron Leader 'Count' Ciano as his navigator, to observe the No. 5 Group daylight raid on the fighter base at Deelan in

Holland. In a letter to the *Aeroplane Monthly* magazine in June 1977, Charles Owen stated that the Lightning was supposed to be used strictly for trials and 'How Gibson took it to Deelan is another story.' Sadly, he did not elaborate upon this comment.

It has also been claimed that shortly after the flight to Deelan, Gibson managed to undertake some dive-bombing training in a de Havilland Mosquito. His tutor was Wing Commander John Woodroffe DSO, DFC, AFC, an experienced target marker and Controller who was based at Coningsby. Sadly, John Woodroffe died in a B-47 US Air Force crash in the United States in October 1957 and he left no known record of his wartime exploits.

Exactly how much dive-bombing training was undertaken is unclear and it was probably not a great deal, but it is clear Gibson wanted to return to operations and as a Controller or low-level target marker.

A few days later, on 18 August, Gibson again flew a P-38 Lightning, this time with Squadron Leader Howard to observe a raid on Fécamp in France. Guy Gibson was inching his way back towards a full operational sortie.

Gibson returned safely, but having watched the bomber crews in action, he must have been desperate to take a more active part in the bombing campaign.

The fact Cochrane had allowed Gibson to fly over occupied enemy territory, only allowed him to push the boundary even further. Gibson had shown his commanders that he could satisfactorily fly a twin-engine aircraft on an operational flight and in his own opinion he probably believed it was now only a small step towards his full participation in a major raid.

Although Gibson was clearly stepping up his flying schedule, he still had his duties as the Base Air Staff Officer (BASO) and the following day (19 August), he flew to Swinderby as a member of the No. 5 Group Operational Research Unit.

Over the years, many people have considered Ralph Cochrane and Arthur Harris to be the main personalities connected with the build-up to Gibson's final fatal flight, but there is one more man who may have been involved in some way. That man was the Commanding Officer of No. 54 Base, Air Commodore Alfred Sharp.

Alfred Sharp was a very experienced pilot and commanding officer, but after flying as a bomber pilot in the early part of the war, he was promoted and sent to the US Army Air Force as an RAF liaison officer.

Air Commodore Sharp was in many ways just like Guy Gibson and desperate to play his part in the war. As an RAF liaison officer, he managed to get aboard at least three American B-17 operations over France and Germany, reportedly taking up a position as a gunner. The Americans were so impressed with the British officer they awarded him a Silver Star and the Legion of Merit.

In February 1944, Alfred Sharp became the Commanding Officer of No. 54 Air Base at Coningsby, but he still wanted more operational flying. With Gibson's old unit No. 617 Squadron based nearby, he managed another flight as a passenger on the raid to the Anthéor Viaduct (which was marked by Leonard Cheshire). Further raids followed throughout early 1944, but word soon reached Bomber Command HQ and he was ordered to immediately stop his operational flights.

In the Arthus Harris papers held at the RAF Museum, Hendon, there is a report from Ralph Cochrane to Harris dated 29 August 1944, just three weeks before Gibson's death. The report concerned Air Commodore Sharp and his desperation for operational flying. Air Vice-Marshal Ralph Cochrane stated:

> 'I wrote to you on 26 June on the subject of Air Commodore Sharp being allowed to go on operational flights. In your reply, you asked me to raise the matter again in two months' time and I am now writing to ask if I can authorise him to fly on three or four operations, so that he may gain further experience of the marking technique which is being developed at his base.'

The report, within three weeks of Gibson's death, is documentary evidence of another senior officer at Coningsby wanting to undertake operational flights, supposedly to learn about target marking. It is also evidence of Ralph Cochrane supporting Sharp, like Gibson, to undertake these flights. This appears in many ways to have been consistent with and parallel to the wishes of Guy Gibson.

Air Vice-Marshal Cochrane concluded his report, stating that Sharp had flown twenty operations during the beginning of the war on Blenheims, many of them particularly hazardous. He had flown others since that time and if it had not been for postings, he would have been considered an outstanding bomber pilot. Cochrane therefore wished to re-submit a recommendation that Alfred Sharp be awarded the Distinguished Service Order. There is a scribbled pencil note on the report which states: 'Ans.

by telephone' and the initials AH (Arthur Harris). Whatever was discussed is unclear, but two months after the death of Guy Gibson on 10 November 1944, the award of Alfred Sharp's DSO appeared in the *London Gazette.*

There is no doubt Alfred Sharp was a kindred spirit for Gibson, but did he play a part in the final flight himself or does this say more about the consent and actions of Cochrane and Harris?

On one of Air Vice-Marshal Cochrane's visits to Coningsby, Gibson reportedly pressed him once again for permission to fly operations. This time, the No. 5 Group AOC told him he would need adequate training if he was to take part in any operations. Unfortunately, there is no evidence Guy Gibson ever received any specialist training before his final flight, apart from his few flights with John Woodroffe.

Although Guy Gibson was an experienced and skilled pilot with a mammoth amount of courage, he was now at the centre of a specialised low-level target marking section within No. 5 Group. He had no operational experience of target marking or controlling himself and only a few practice flights in a Mosquito with Johnny Woodroffe, to count as training in dive-bombing.

It is widely accepted that Guy Gibson was a skilled night-time, low-level pilot and he could control a small force like that on the Dams raid in May 1943, but he had no in-depth training on dropping target markers or controlling a force of 200 or more bombers. In addition, although he had flown the Mosquito aircraft used by No. 627 Squadron for the task of low-level target marking and controlling a number of times, he had not undertaken specific conversion training and what direction he had received, was somewhat ad-hoc.

The No. 627 Squadron pilots and navigators, when they transferred to No. 5 Group in April 1944, were already skilled Pathfinders, but they spent many days and weeks, dropping practice bombs and flares day and night on the Wainfleet ranges while perfecting their low-level flying skills.

At higher altitudes the navigator would enter the glazed nose of the Mosquito and drop their TIs using the aircrafts bombsight, but at low-level, the navigator stayed in his seat just behind the pilot, who often dropped the TIs himself. In addition, No. 627 Squadron crews often flew at a lower-altitudes, making their navigation another difficult skill to master.

These were the skill sets that were needed for Guy Gibson to undertake any operational flying and act as a target marker or controller with No. 5 Group.

At some point between 20–25 August 1944, Gibson appears to have flown down to London in a final bid to push his case for a return to operations, whether he saw Arthur Harris is unknown.

On 26 August, Gibson flew a P-38 Lightning to Langford Lodge in Northern Ireland so the American engineers could fit a British Gee set to the aircraft for target marking duties; the aircraft evidently still being tested and evaluated for work with No. 627 Squadron.

In late August 1944, navigator Flight Lieutenant James Warwick arrived at Coningsby from No. 1661 Heavy Conversion Unit at Fiskerton, where he had set up a radar navigation section. James Warwick was 'tour expired' from operations with No. 49

Squadron in 1943 and he had received the Distinguished Flying Cross. When he arrived at Coningsby for a non-flying ground role he was accompanied by his fiancé whom he was due to marry. James Warwick had only served on heavy bombers, but he would soon become entwined with Guy Gibson's fate.

According to Hamish Mahaddie in his book *Hamish*, Air Vice-Marshal Ralph Cochrane (author's note: almost certainly at the behest of Harris), agreed to Gibson going on operations, but still with the proviso he attended the Pathfinder Course at RAF Warboys, as well as a short course on the Mosquito, before attempting any low-level target marking or controlling. Mahaddie added that Gibson would, with his skills, have had the ability to undertake this highly dangerous role. He would have also benefitted a great deal from a few hours with the Pathfinder school at RAF Warboys, perhaps with a couple of low-level bombing attacks on the practice range at Wainfleet. However, Gibson stayed away from Warboys and the No. 8 Pathfinder Course, why he chose not to attend is unknown.

RAF Warboys and No. 8 Group had been training their own Pathfinder crews as well as those for No. 5 Group – much to their chagrin – for many months, so there was no issue with Gibson being a No. 5 Group pupil. It was more likely Guy Gibson's ego decided he did not need the specialist training.

On 2 September 1944, Gibson borrowed a de Havilland Mosquito, serial KB213, from No. 627 Squadron. Why he made this flight is unclear, but he flew the aircraft to Wick in Scotland, before going on to RAF Scatsta in the Shetland Isles. Who his unfortunate navigator was is unclear, but they were to have a *hairy* landing at Scatsta, which had a short runway, surrounded by low hills and the sea. Gibson needed all his skill to put the high-speed Mosquito down on the short runway on his third attempt. This Mosquito, serial number KB213, would play a significant role in Gibson's final flight less than three weeks later.

On 7 September, Gibson flew an Airspeed Oxford to take cine film of the surrounding Lincolnshire area. He was accompanied by Wing Commander John Woodroffe again, but three days later on 10 September, the two men flew in a No. 627 Squadron Mosquito, believed to have been DZ633, on a late afternoon raid to Le Havre. The two men took a cine film of the raid on the German held port, but whether Woodroffe or Gibson was piloting the aircraft that day is unclear, but it was probably Gibson.

On 5 September 1944, Leonard Cheshire's Victoria Cross was formally announced in the *London Gazette*. As we have seen, there have been unsubstantiated reports that Gibson was less than impressed with the award of Cheshire's VC, but on 12 September, he took time to write a letter, congratulating him on his award. (This can be viewed at the International Bomber Command Centre in Lincoln.) Leonard Cheshire was being sent out to the Far East to work with the Americans in planning for ending the war with Japan – hence the comments in Gibson's letter. Whether this was a genuine letter of heartfelt congratulations or Gibson had only written it because of his connections to the man via No. 617 Squadron and No. 5 Group is open to debate. He wrote:

> 'My Dear Leonard,
>
> 'Just a line to congratulate you most heartily on your very well-earned VC. It was a mighty fine effort and has received universal praise. It is a great show for 617.

> 'I don't know if this will ever get to you, but don't reply anyway, as you will get a lot of these.
>
> 'See you out there.
>
> Yours ever, Guy Gibson.'

The comment 'See you out there', was a clear reference to Guy Gibson wanting to fly against the Japanese in the Far East once the war in Europe was concluded, something he expected to happen in the coming weeks.

Leonard Cheshire only received the letter when he arrived in Delhi, India, sadly Gibson was killed before he received it.

It is possible Leonard Cheshire, with his previous command of No. 617 Squadron, his pioneering efforts in low-level target marking and now the award of the VC, was an issue for Guy Gibson. If he was even remotely upset, he must have been angered by the newspaper headlines on the 8th and 9th September, which proclaimed:

> 'Greatest bomber pilot gets VC.' said the *Gloucestershire Echo.*
>
> 'RAF's Pathfinder genius gets VC.' said the *Derby Daily Telegraph.*
>
> 'Chesh is second to none, greatest bomber pilot in the world.' said the *Daily Record.*
>
> 'Greatest bomber pilot of all, sacrificed his promotion to continue leading raids.' said the *Daily News* in London.

These were just a few of the headlines splashed across the United Kingdom's newspapers. Guy Gibson must have wondered what had happened to him, less than sixteen months before, he had been the greatest of all bomber pilots, but now he seemed to have been forgotten by the journalists. Whether these headlines pushed Gibson towards his final flight just ten days later is a matter of conjecture and debate, but they probably didn't help his decision-making processes.

Over the next few days in mid-September, Gibson flew twice more on non-operational flights, this time in Lancasters from Coningsby.

On 13 September, Gibson flew an Airspeed Oxford with Wing Commander Simpson – another senior controller at Coningsby. They took some cine camera footage of an accompanying Lancaster before they returned home. Gibson was certainly surrounding himself with the experienced controllers such as Woodroffe, Simpson and Charles Owen and his appetite for operational flying had been whetted, but it had not been satisfied. As an operational commander, he wanted more than a bit part and cine camera filming.

The Allied armies continued to advance through Belgium and into Holland and on 17 September, Operation Market Garden was launched. This plan involved the dropping of a carpet of paratroopers from the United States, Britain and Poland across Holland at Eindhoven, Nijmegen and Arnhem. A series of bridges were to be captured and an armoured division (Thirty Corps) would then link-up with the various elements, before a push was made into the industrial heartland of the Ruhr Valley, an area the RAF bomber crews knew as 'Happy Valley' due to its considerable defences.

News of Operation Market Garden was another element that probably sat heavily on the shoulders of the impatient Guy Gibson. Here was a plan that if successful, could end the war by Christmas 1944. Although most people would rejoice at such a conclusion, it undoubtedly caused dismay to Guy Gibson, as it would undoubtedly lessen the chances of his return to operations.

Unknown to Gibson at the time, Operation Market Garden would become something of a heroic failure, more commonly known now as *A Bridge Too Far,* the British elements would become surrounded by a SS Panzer Division, leading to its near annihilation. So bad were the losses, Air Vice-Marshal Donald Bennett even asked Harris if his No. 8 Group Pathfinder Force could be used to drop supplies to the beleaguered British paras. The offer was not accepted by the Commander-in-Chief.

On 18 September, John Searby visited Coningsby and met with his old friend Guy Gibson. In his book, Searby says Gibson was not very enthusiastic about his appointment to the Base Commander's Staff. Gibson was itching to get back on operations and after they had lunch together in the Officers' Mess, he took Searby into a hangar to see a de Havilland Mosquito. Gibson told Searby that he intended to use the aircraft when doing the odd sortie, but exactly what type of sortie he meant was not disclosed.

John Searby recalled Gibson having something of his old spirit present during their final meeting and their time together was a happy one. However, the following day would sadly be Guy Gibson's last day on earth.

Chapter Seven

No. 5 Group Pathfinders

It is worth pausing at this juncture to consider the role Guy Gibson would be performing when he died on 19 September 1944. Gibson would act as the Controller (usually known in No. 8 Group as a Master Bomber), for a force of No. 5 Group Lancasters on a raid into Germany. This was a specialist role which required a high degree of skill, both as a pilot, a communicator and as a dedicated target marking controller. The role was usually undertaken by an experienced and highly trained bomber pilot, someone who had received extra training, as well as experience as a target marker himself.

As previously noted, Bomber Command set up their original Pathfinder unit in August 1942. Eventually, they became a Group in their own right – No. 8 Group (PFF), but they took squadrons and crews from other Bomber Command Groups to form this elite cadre of airmen. Initially, Air Marshal Arthur Harris was not very keen on the formation, but eventually he relented and the Pathfinder units played an integral part in marking targets across Germany and occupied Europe for the bomber force.

Heavy bombers such as the Lancaster and Halifax would mark targets with a variety of tools including flares, other incendiary devices and specially developed target markers known as TIs. The flares and TIs were usually dropped with the aid of electronic navigation systems such as Gee and the H2S radar system. The No. 8 Group Pathfinder units operated at medium altitude ahead of the main bomber force, identifying and marking the aiming point for the bombers.

As already mentioned, in February 1944, No. 5 Group's Air Officer Commanding, Air Vice-Marshal Ralph Cochrane, spoke with Air Marshal Harris about target marking. Thanks to the commander of No. 617 Squadron – Wing Commander Leonard Cheshire's experiments and ingenuity – it was believed fast agile aircraft such as the de Havilland Mosquito could accurately mark a target at low-level for the main bomber force. Cheshire, with the assistance of Harold 'Mick' Martin, had proven that low-level target marking could succeed, with a raid on the Gnome-Rhone aero engine factory at Limoges in France. Using Lancasters rather than Mosquitos, they dropped a marker followed by incendiaries before the main force bombed from a higher altitude. With this evidence, Cochrane convinced the Commander-in-Chief of Bomber Command that they could mark targets in Berlin from just fifty feet above the roof tops. Having listened to Ralph Cochrane, Harris telephoned Air Vice-Marshal Donald Bennett, the AOC of No. 8 Group (Pathfinder Force) to discuss the idea.

Donald Bennett pointed out to Air Marshal Harris that target indicators (TIs) dropped at a low altitude could not be seen through a cloud layer by a bomber force above the clouds. For this reason, No. 8 Group used spot flares and other devices to mark aiming points, their markers slowly descending above the covering cloud layer so they could be seen by the bomber stream. In addition, Bennett, from his own experience, believed it was virtually impossible at night to accurately map-read at low altitude and identify the target. He added that he agreed the method could be used in a thinly populated area, but not a major city like Berlin. Having given his views, the Commander-in-Chief promptly concluded the telephone call.

Later, Bennett was summoned to Bomber Command Headquarters to see Harris face to face. Upon arrival, he was ordered to immediately release the Lancasters of Nos. 83 and 97 Squadrons from his Pathfinder Group, and send them to Cochrane's No. 5 Group. In addition, the Mosquitos of No. 627 Squadron were also to be transferred to Cochrane's group. Bennett was informed that No. 5 Group would now employ Cochrane's idea of low-level target marking. Bennett was less than impressed and believed it constituted a metaphorical 'slap in the face' for his Pathfinder Group. To make matters worse, No. 8 Group would be required to train all Pathfinder crews for Ralph Cochrane's No. 5 Group, at their own training unit at RAF Warboys in Cambridgeshire.

From Spring to September 1944, the three squadrons would undertake a number of operations, developing and perfecting this new low-level target marking ideology. The three squadrons were initially unimpressed with having to leave the dedicated Pathfinder Force, but eventually they made their mark with low-level marking and were still allowed to wear their distinctive Pathfinder badges. This was the relatively new structure Guy Gibson found when he arrived at Coningsby on 4 August 1944.

Although Guy Gibson was fully conversant with the use of Pathfinders and their tactics, having experienced their development and use in 1942-1943, great strides had been made in the use of the technology since his last operational flight in May 1943. In fact, Gibson's last direct experience of night-time target marking and Pathfinder techniques, was his final raid to Stuttgart on 11 March 1943, eighteen months before what would become his final flight.

Apart from the different altitude from which target indicators were dropped, the new force started to develop its own terminology. The man in charge of directing No. 8 Group Pathfinder markers and raids was called the Master Bomber, but No. 5 Group soon called their man 'the Controller.'

No. 5 Group's in-depth records for target marking can still be viewed in the UK National Archives under the reference AIR 14/868. One document written towards the end of the war was marked *Secret* and titled: *5 Group Marking Procedure*, gives details of No. 5 Group's marking techniques.

The report states that the following factors, peculiar to different types of target markers (TIs), must be borne in mind when planning an attack:

1. Red TIs should be used for all priority marking, particularly in an incendiary attack, as Green TIs are difficult to distinguish when burning amongst 4lb incendiaries.
2. Green TIs may be used as a primary marker, or as a priority marker in a high explosive attack, provided long delay fused bombs are used.
3. Yellow TIs are unsuitable for primary or secondary marking, but can be used for confirmation of accurate, or scrubbing of 'wide' markers.

Primary blind target markers were used by specially trained Lancaster crews, (i.e. those of Nos. 83 and 97 Squadrons) using H2S radar to drop green TIs in the target area. The green target indicators would act as a datum point for the Mosquito markers (i.e. No. 627 Squadron) and for visual flare dropping. As a last resort, they could be used as a marking point for the main bombing if the visual bombing had been impossible.

The same Lancasters could also drop flares to illuminate the target area by dropping long sticks of parachute supported white flares.

The two differing RAF Pathfinder Forces, by September 1944 (namely Nos. 5 and 8 Groups), used highly developed techniques with cutting-edge technology to mark their targets. Various different systems, flares and markers were utilised, but for Gibson's final sortie, we shall concentrate on low-level marking with ground target indicators and not those used at higher altitudes.

Target indicators were pyrotechnic devices, usually housed in a 250lb bomb casing, although larger devices up to 1,000lb and even a 4,000lb device were used.

A target indicator held a number of pyrotechnic 'candles' which at a predetermined altitude, usually via a barometric fuse, were ejected and ignited above the target or on the ground depending on the type of device used. The target indicator would burn for between 3 to 35 minutes depending upon the number of candles it carried and the frequency at which they were ejected. If they landed in water, this would instantly extinguish them.

The conveyance of combustible target indicators could be dangerous, and on occasions target indicators were known to have *hung-up* and fail to drop from the aircraft. This could be very dangerous, especially with an armed pyrotechnic hanging inside the bomb bay of an aircraft made predominantly of wood (i.e. the de Havilland Mosquito). To deal with such eventualities, Pathfinder crews were trained to eject the *hung-up* device and its supporting cradle from the bomb bay to avoid bringing home an unsteady target indicator.

In the summer of 1944, No. 627 Squadron was primarily using the B16, B22 and B24 types of target indicators. These contained various types of candles, with the type B16 holding 11x instant ignition candles, 45x delayed and 4x explosive candles. These were either red, green or yellow in colour. This gave a cascade of 60x candles on striking the target and giving it a burn time duration of about twelve minutes.

In comparison, the type B24 device had 8x instant ignition candles, 48x delayed and 4x explosive candles in red, green and yellow. This gave an increased cascade of 60x candles, but with a burn time duration of about twelve minutes. In essence, this meant there was a slight variation in intensity over the twelve minutes period of burn time.

Ground marking was often undertaken with the primary blind marking aircraft (i.e. Lancasters using Gee or H2S radar) dropping long-burning green TIs. The mean point of the visible green TIs would then be assessed by the Controller and marked with red TIs by the Mosquitos. To indicate and emphasise correct target marking, yellow TIs, or a white TI which flashed dots and dashes, could be used by the backup marker aircraft and the Controller.

In addition, No. 627 Squadron's Mosquitos would often carry incendiary bombs, their own illumination flares, Red Spot flares and Wanganui flares. The Wanganui flares were used when the target was covered in cloud and ground marking would be ineffective. Red Spot flares were another 250lb device containing a cotton wool sock impregnated with a mixture that would ignite at a predetermined altitude. As it floated slowly down to earth, it gave off a bright red flame for fifteen to twenty minutes and continued to burn when it hit the ground.

In certain conditions, the Lancaster illumination Pathfinder aircraft would drop flares to enable the Mosquitos of No. 627 Squadron to drop their ground markers from low-level. Once this was completed, the Controller would call in the main bomber force, directing them to bomb certain markers by identifying their colour as the target. This latter tactic was the type to be used in Guy Gibson's final operation and controlled by him, although as we shall see, that night it incorporated a much more complicated plan.

The No. 5 Group Pathfinder report added a section titled: *Mosquito Markers.* This stated:

> 'Visual markers are dropped by Mosquitos in a dive from 3-4,000 feet down to 800 feet. Markers are released visually and although no form of sight is used, an average accuracy of about 200 yards can be expected.'

Later in the report, there is a section on Master Bombers, or Controllers as the Group called them:

All attacks are directed by a Master Bomber normally flying in a Mosquito, who is responsible for assessing the accuracy of marking and has full authority to:

- Stop the bombing.
- Order all aircraft to return to base before the attack is completed.
- Change the direction of the attack.
- Alter the flight plan in any way he considers necessary.
- Amend the Marking Plan to suit the weather conditions encountered at the target.

All orders are broadcast on VHF/RT but to overcome the chances of unserviceability of VHF in main force aircraft, the Master Bomber/Controller's orders are relayed on W/T by a link aircraft of the marker force. (i.e. No. 83 and 97 Squadron Lancasters).

(N.B. It is interesting to note that although No. 5 Group used the term Controller, this report still called them a Master Bomber.)

This is a very short summary of what No. 5 Group's Pathfinder units were doing in 1944–1945. There are a number of other tactics, but these are the main areas of concern when considering the final sortie and ultimately the death of Guy Gibson.

By September 1944, No. 5 Group had been assessing the merits of different aircraft for Controller duties. Although No. 627 Squadron were already using the de Havilland Mosquito, they were also testing the P-51 Mustang and the P-38 Lockheed Lightning, which Gibson had flown a number of times in the weeks leading up to his death.

It is interesting to note that in another No. 5 Group report, dated 2 September 1944, just seventeen days before Gibson's fatal flight, it states the Mosquito was fast and manoeuvrable, but was unstable in the air. This led to a pilot being unable to give his undivided attention to controlling. In addition, the cockpit was cramped and the layout of instruments was poor for a Controller.

The report minuted and signed by Air Officer Commanding Air Vice-Marshal Ralph Cochrane, reached the conclusion the P-38 Lockheed Lightning was much more suitable than the Mosquito for controlling duties.

An earlier No. 5 Group report dated 21 April 1944, was titled: *Operational Roles of Squadrons.* This detailed report covered the three Pathfinder units, including the Mosquitos of No. 627 Squadron.

The report repeated the low-level ground marking tactics of the Mosquitos, but added that the first target marker to identify the target aiming point, should inform the Controller over the R/T with the code words 'Tally-ho.' Except for the code words Tally-ho, plain language should be used over the R/T between the Mosquito target markers and the Controller. It then added clearly and importantly, 'Considerable practice will be necessary if messages are to be clear and concise.' This sentence is worth remembering for later in this book.

No. 627 Squadron's operations from mid-August to late September 1944, are contained within their Operations Record

Books ref: AIR 27/2149 & 2150 in the UK National Archives. Full details are contained within the appendix at the end of this book, but in summary, it is clear their operations were quite simple compared to that which Guy Gibson undertook on his final flight.

On 15 August, the squadron marked daylight targets at Deelan and Gilze-Rijen Luftwaffe airfields in Holland. Gibson was flying a P-38 Lightning in an observation role on the Deelan raid. Three days later, No. 627 Squadron dropped smoke markers on L'Isle-Adam during another daylight raid.

On the night of 25-26 August, No. 627 Squadron marked the target at Darmstadt in Germany, using red TIs. Yellow TIs were to be used as a cancellation signal if required.

Further simple daylight raids followed on 31 August and 3-5 September.

On the night of 9-10 of September, No. 627 squadron marked the aiming point for a raid on Mönchengladbach. This raid would be repeated on Guy Gibson's last flight ten days later. No. 627 Squadron once again used type B22 red TIs to mark the aiming point, backed-up by the other Mosquitos with loads of incendiaries. As such it was a relatively simple and straightforward method of marking.

On 11 September, the squadron visited Darmstadt again, dropping a series of type B16, B22 and B24 1,000lb red target indicators. The Mosquitos also carried incendiary bombs, Red Spot flares and Wanganui flares.

Night-time raids to Stuttgart on 12-13 September and Bremerhaven on 18-19 September, followed with the usual standard marking procedures being followed. The Stuttgart raid used illumination flares and green markers dropped by the Pathfinder Lancaster units, before the Mosquitos marked with red TIs. Once again, the Mosquitos also carried Wanganui and Red Spot flares for use if required. Bremerhaven, six nights later, used a very similar plan and both raids were deemed to have been relatively successful.

After Guy Gibson's final flight on the night of 19-20 September, No. 627 Squadron undertook operations to the Dortmund-Ems Canal and Münster, on the night of the 23-24 September. This time they employed just red TIs with a backup of yellow TIs as this was their normal practice. Unfortunately, due to poor visibility and camouflaging of the target, many aircraft failed to identify the aiming point and did not drop their target indicators.

Four nights later, No. 627 Squadron visited Karlsruhe and Kaiserslautern. This time, due to low cloud and poor visibility, low-level marking was not possible and they were ordered to back up the H2S Lancaster dropped green TIs. The raid had varying results.

This series of target marking operations illustrates how No. 627 Squadron routinely marked targets for the No. 5 Group bomber force in the summer of 1944. They had been following a set process as highlighted in the No. 5 Group report discussed at the start of this chapter. This process was not completely rigid and it gave the Controller some autonomy in directing the markers and the bomber force when it arrived. However, as we shall see, the plan for the raid from which Guy Gibson failed to return, would be unlike any of the previous or subsequent target marking sorties of No. 627 Squadron, much to their confusion and in some cases annoyance. This would lead to questions about who created the plan for the raid.

It is worth considering again, that while he was a very experienced pilot, Gibson's last two operations with No. 106 Squadron were on 26 February and 11 March 1943. Although targets started to be marked in mid-August 1942, by March 1943, the TI process was still in its relative infancy and Gibson had never been a Master Bomber or Controller; although some would argue he had taken on a form of Controlling role during the Dams raid, circling overhead and directing affairs.

A comparison of the No. 8 Group Pathfinder records against Gibson's own flying logbook, indicates that he took part in at least eleven raids during which target marking was utilised. However, five of these raids were made against the much more lightly defended Italian cities and one or two of the German targets had problems with the marking process.

In summary, Guy Gibson, with no dedicated Pathfinder training at Warboys and no operational experience of pathfinding techniques since March 1943, was a complete novice as far as Controller duties were concerned; yet on the 19 September 1944, he set out to undertake this important role with disastrous results.

Chapter Eight

The Build up to 19 September 1944

On the morning of 19 September 1944, a meeting took place in the Operations Room at Bomber Command Headquarters near High Wycombe. A group of staff officers, experts in meteorology and intelligence, waited for the arrival of the Commander-in-Chief, Air Marshal Arthur 'Bomber' Harris. This scene had been repeated many times of the past few years and took a very familiar routine for those present.

After general housekeeping matters and a review of the previous night-time raid to Bremerhaven, Air Marshal Harris had to decide what targets would be hit that night. After a number of months supporting the Allied invasion of France, Harris was now allowed to attack a number of German cities, in effect a return to his old strategic bombing campaign and the dismantling of Germany industry.

In mid-September, the British and Canadian armies had advanced to a position near the Belgian-Dutch border, while the Americans were moving eastwards in southern Belgium and France.

The Allied High Command, desperate to end the war, authorised Field Marshal Montgomery to undertake Operation Market Garden. This was his own plan and called for the mass drop of paratroopers around Eindhoven, as well as Nijmegen and Arnhem. The plan was for the paratroopers to capture several key bridges over the Rhine and various adjacent waterways, before an armoured thrust linked up with them and ultimately headed into the industrial Ruhr Valley. This it was hoped, would curtail the war.

The operation started on 17 September 1944, but the armoured units belonging to XXX Corps, were having problems smashing their way through the German defences to link-up with the airborne forces at the bridges. On the morning of 19 September, it was clear there was an impending disaster with the encircled British paras at Arnhem in particular danger.

The area between the German Ruhr and the front line in Holland was now packed with the 9th SS Panzer Division, as well as various retreating military units from Belgium. Many of these units had significant anti-aircraft defences in the form of the formidable rapid-fire 20mm cannon, many of them mounted in a quadruple system on tracked vehicles or towed units. Like the 40mm Bofors gun used by the British, these weapons were deadly against low-flying aircraft.

In addition, there were also the Luftwaffe airfields at Deelen and Gilze-Rijen bristling with their own anti-aircraft guns, as well as fighter aircraft. The area was now a deathtrap for low-flying aircraft, as many of the paratroop dropping transport aircraft and gliders found to their cost. During 17-19 September 1944, the RAF lost seven Dakotas, nine Short Stirling glider tugs and sixteen Spitfires, Mustangs and Tempests to low-level flak. This figure does not include aircraft lost by the American forces around Nijmegen and Eindhoven, or British glider losses which were considerable. On 20 September, No. 29 Squadron lost a Mosquito intruder which crashed near Arnhem, the pilot allegedly being blinded by the searchlights.

According to the weather reports on 19 September, Northern Europe was dominated by an anti-cyclone to the north-east of the United Kingdom. Low pressure was now moving in from the Atlantic Ocean, but the meteorological teams believed this front of rain and cloud would not arrive until after the night's raids. On the morning of the nineteenth, there was some fog and low cloud over the various bomber airfields in Yorkshire and Lincolnshire, but this was expected to disperse by early afternoon. Over the Continent, there was some low cloud, but many areas were clear with good weather.

The main concern for the Bomber Command planners was the probability the fog would return after midnight and hinder any aircraft returning home to their airfields in Eastern England. Fearful of this, Harris wanted his bombers home before the fog came down and he therefore decided against sending raids to the far-flung parts of Germany. Any raids, he decreed, would have to be home by midnight to avoid the fog.

It was decided that a large force would make an attack in daylight during the afternoon of 19 September, while Mosquitos from No. 8 Group's Light Night Striking Force would visit Berlin.

No. 5 Group were to make another night-time attack on the city of Bremerhaven. The Group were directed to prepare 200 of their Lancasters, backed up by a number of Lancasters from No. 1 Group for the raid on the port.

The weather situation continued to change by the hour and by 11:00hrs (BST), the large daylight raid planned for that afternoon was cancelled. Later still, the No. 8 Group Mosquito raid to Berlin was also cancelled and they were redirected to attack Brunswick. No. 5 Group's raid to Bremerhaven was given the go-ahead and the ground crews calculated the necessary fuel required for the mission, while the armourers armed and loaded the bombs and target indicators.

A de Havilland Mosquito of 1409 Meteorological Flight had been dispatched to check the weather over Holland and Western Germany, and upon return to RAF Wyton the crew reported fine weather with some stratus and altocumulus clouds. Upon receipt of this information the raid to Bremerhaven appeared to be 'on', but other reports to the south over the English Channel and Northern France indicated the weather had started to deteriorate. Further weather forecasts later indicated that fog would envelope No. 5 Group's airfields in Lincolnshire around midnight and the early hours of 20 September. The Bomber Command planners therefore decided, mid-afternoon, to cancel the Bremerhaven raid and redirect No. 5 Group against Rheydt and Mönchengladbach, which was closer to the German-Dutch border and England.

This change of plan was a late order and the ground crews worked to reconfigure their aircraft, while the planners at No. 5 Group HQ at Morton Hall near RAF Swinderby worked on a new route and timings. Once the new orders and instructions were ready, they were passed on to the designated individual stations and squadrons for the raid, which included Coningsby.

Mönchengladbach had been visited by No. 5 Group on the night of 9-10 September. The order and summary for that raid contained within UK National Archives file reference

AIR 27/2150, gives a bleak objective: 'Destroy town centre Mönchengladbach.' The raid and target marking, which was controlled by the experienced Squadron Leader Charles Owen, was deemed to be something of a success, but the target was not completely destroyed, therefore the new orders were given for another visit.

The new orders from Bomber Command (also contained in UK archives reference AIR 27/2150) were just as harsh and blunt, their objective stating: 'To complete the destruction of Mönchengladbach and Rheydt.'

The target marking plan was very different to the previous raid on Mönchengladbach and other recent night-time attacks, in fact it was much more complicated. There would be three aiming points, using three different coloured target indicators:

- The Red TI aiming point would be in the centre of Rheydt.
- The Green TI aiming point was an industrial area of Mönchengladbach.
- The Yellow TI aiming point was an area close to the railway station in Mönchengladbach.

This new plan was different in a number of ways. First of all, three aiming points utilising three different coloured target indicators was unusual. Normally, red target indicators were used for the primary target and its aiming point, but in this case, there would be three different primary aiming points using three different coloured TIs. In addition, the order directed that if there were any problems targeting Mönchengladbach (with the green and yellow TIs), the Controller would direct all aircraft to bomb Rheydt and the red TI marked aiming point.

The three aiming points would be illuminated with flares dropped by the Lancasters of Nos. 83 and 97 Squadrons at 21:35hrs (BST). This would allow the Mosquitos of No. 627 Squadron to identify the three aiming points and mark them with the requisite coloured ground marker TIs. Once successfully marked, the Controller would call in the main bomber force in three waves to strike the three separate aiming points, this taking place at 'H-hour', in this case 21:45hrs (BST), just ten minutes after the initial illumination by flares.

Who gave instructions for this complicated target marking plan is unclear, but it came from the No. 5 Group HQ and may or may not have involved Air Vice-Marshal Ralph Cochrane. The question is, did Headquarters know at the time, who the Controller would be on this particular raid?

At 17:45hrs (BST) the aircrews of No. 5 Group went to their briefing rooms. They were given details of their targets and their routes to and from them. The main bomber stream was routed via a waypoint at Clacton on Sea, then across the North Sea to a point between Ostend and Dunkirk. It then turned near Charleroi in Belgium towards Germany. After crossing the German border near Aachen, the various squadrons would head for their individual aiming points. It was planned that a diversionary force from No. 100 Group would head further into Germany dropping 'Window' to confuse the German radars, while transmitting jamming noises to confuse the enemy night-fighters and their controllers.

It is said, No. 627 Squadron's Mosquito crews were surprised at their own briefing, when it was revealed, Guy Gibson would be Controller for the raid. After his recent 'engagement' with some of the airmen in No. 627 Squadron's bar, Guy Gibson was undoubtedly an unwelcome addition to the raid. Many crews probably questioning why he was going along and not one of the other, more experienced controllers, or even their own unit commander Wing Commander Curry?

After hitting their targets, the main bomber force from No. 5 Group would head across Holland and out over the North Sea for home. They were routed with a dog leg course to take them south of the combat area of Market Garden around Eindhoven and Arnhem. This, it was hoped, would avoid the heavy fighting and the considerable number of flak guns in that area.

The Mosquitos of No. 627 Squadron would take-off after the Lancaster squadrons, their higher speed allowing them to overtake the heavy bombers in time to mark the aiming points. They would head directly to and from the target across Holland.

It is said that when the briefers disclosed that there would be three different aiming points with different coloured TIs, it was met with some incredulity and confusion right across No. 5 Group and not only from the Mosquito crews. As already mentioned, that incredulity increased when they were informed the identity of their Controller for the night. Instead of Wing Commander John Woodroffe, Squadron Leader Charles Owen, or even their own squadron commander Wing Commander Curry, it would be Wing Commander 'Dambuster' Guy Gibson. The Deputy Controller would be Squadron Leader Ron Churcher, an experienced No. 627 Squadron man with two tours of operations under his belt, one of which had been with Gibson on No. 106 Squadron back in 1942.

Nine Mosquitos would make up three flights. Each flight of three aircraft would have a different coloured target indicator assigned to them. Each flight was given an identity according to the marker colour: i.e. Red 1 (Squadron Leader Ron Churcher), Red 2, Red 3, Green 1, Green 2 and so on.

In his book *Mosquito Men*, David Price says that some of the crews who had their doubts about Gibson, 'Felt things were being arranged so he could be seen as orchestrator in chief of a complex target marking procedure and thereby enjoy another moment of glory.' He added that No. 627 Squadron crews knew the station commander Air Commodore Alfred Sharp was away and maybe, Gibson had taken advantage of this opportunity to make himself the Controller.

There is also the question of whether Gibson had a hand in the target marking plan? Is it possible Guy Gibson now saw a way to enhance his own reputation, devising, leading and superseding the marking system originally devised by Leonard Cheshire? Could he have been at the No. 5 Group HQ mid-afternoon and helped devise the plan? Or did 'someone' else make this plan, possibly after a previous meeting or discussion with Gibson?

Whatever happened, as we have seen, it appears Air Vice-Marshal Ralph Cochrane and even 'Bomber' Harris probably had their part in deciding that Gibson would be allowed to go on this operational sortie. Whether they decided he could be the Controller is unclear to this day, especially as we know

Ralph Cochrane had told Gibson he had to join the Pathfinder course at Warboys, before going on any operational sortie.

Exactly when Guy Gibson was informed he could go on this operation is unknown. It is also unclear as to when he was told he would be the Controller, or if he alone decided he was going to take on the role that night. It is possible Gibson had known for some time that he would be the Controller that night, or he decided the day before, after his meeting with John Searby at Coningsby.

In his book *Born Leader*, Alan Cooper claims that Guy Gibson took the Mosquito from the hangar at Coningsby for a night flying test on the morning of the raid (19 September). This is believed to have been the same aircraft he had shown John Searby the day before, but it was unserviceable. The controllers based at Coningsby, such as Charles Owen and John Woodroffe, usually flew from their own airfield, but this aircraft was now unserviceable so a call was made to No. 627 Squadron at nearby Woodhall Spa. They were told the Controller (Gibson) would drive over and collect a spare Mosquito.

If it is correct, Gibson had made the night flying test that morning, so either he was testing the aircraft for another pilot, or he was due to fly it and act as the Controller on the now cancelled raid to Bremerhaven. If he was to undertake the role at Bremerhaven, that would have been a much longer flight and he would have spent a much longer period of time over enemy occupied territory. This raises questions again about who was sanctioning his participation that night and what his orders were?

Guy Gibson is known to have received a telephone call from Eve that afternoon. She later recalled that he sounded irritated and she assumed he was therefore too busy to talk. He asked her if there was anything wrong, but when she said she only wanted to talk to him, he told her he would call her the following day. It was the last time they would talk to one another.

Whoever made the decisions and created the target marking plan, Guy Gibson was about to actively participate in his first operational flight in sixteen months. Not only had procedures and technology changed considerably within that time frame, he had not controlled a squadron in the air, let alone target markers and a bomber force numbering in their hundreds. He had also never dropped a target marker himself.

In addition to this lack of experience, Gibson had no dedicated navigator of his own and he had only a few hours flying time logged on the de Havilland Mosquito.

Gibson was to have been assisted by a No. 627 Squadron navigator who was recently 'tour-expired', and it has been claimed that man was Pilot Officer Dai Thomas. He was a very experienced Mosquito navigator having flown with Nos. 139 and 627 Squadrons since 1943, but he is said to have reported sick with a heavy cold at the last moment on the day of the Rheydt-Mönchengladbach raid.

Whether Dai Thomas knew he was to fly that night with Guy Gibson is unknown, but it appears he never told his son Michael about this. (An account of Dai Thomas, and provided by his son Michael, can be found on the website raf-pathfindersarchive.com) If correct, a simple cold could have saved Dai Thomas's life that night.

Dai Thomas had last flown with his regular pilot, New Zealander Flying Officer Parlato, on 11 September on the Darmstadt raid. After recovering from his sickness, he was posted on 4 October to the Air Crew Allocation Centre at Brackla near Inverness and survived the war.

Navigator Flight Lieutenant Donald Bowes was also allegedly tipped-off by his regular pilot and associate of Gibson – Charles Owen. Speaking with the author in 2024, Charles Owen's son, Oliver, said he had been told by Bowes's daughter, that her father was advised by Charles Owen to avoid his own room and the Officers' Mess that afternoon, as Gibson was looking for a navigator. This was confirmed and corroborated by the daughter of Bowes in April 2024, when the author spoke with her.

It is clear on this apparent evidence, that no one wanted to fly with Guy Gibson. He therefore approached Squadron Leader James Warwick, who had only recently arrived at Coningsby and was tour-expired. James Warwick was a very experienced navigator, but a man who had never flown in a de Havilland Mosquito. Whether he volunteered or was caught unawares, cornered and ordered to be Gibson's navigator is another mystery to this day.

At about 18:30hrs (BST) Gibson and Warwick were driven the short distance from Coningsby to Woodhall Spa, possibly by Charles Owen, but this cannot be confirmed. Upon arrival at the dispersal, they were told that Mosquito serial number KB213 had been prepared for them. This was the Mosquito used by Charles Owen for the Mönchengladbach raid on 9-10 September and again for the raid on Stuttgart on 12-13 September. In addition,

Owen had flown it locally three times that month, without any reported issues.

The Mosquito (KB213) was loaded with four 250lb target indicators, one green, one red, one yellow and one extra, as well as a number of flares. This was the normal complement for the Controller's aircraft and differed from the machines of No. 627 Squadron, which had dedicated, red, green or yellow TIs in their bomb bays. The Controller's aircraft had all three colours, as this would allow him to mark each of the three aiming points if he was required to do so.

Upon being told of his designated aircraft, Guy Gibson immediately rejected it and demanded another. Why he dismissed this Mosquito is a mystery to this day, could Charles Owen have mentioned a minor technical problem with the aircraft on his earlier raids, or was it just superstition based on the aircraft's serial number? Gibson had flown the same aircraft to Scotland just a few weeks before so superstition appears unlikely.

After some allegedly heated discussion, which is believed to have included the No. 627 Squadron CO Wing Commander Curry, it was finally agreed that Gibson would take Mosquito KB267 (marked AZ-E). The crew of that aircraft, Flight Lieutenants Peter Mallender and Wallace Gaunt, were less than happy. They, like all crews, had prepared and checked their Mosquito that afternoon and they were now being displaced and given the machine rejected by Gibson, only an hour before take-off.

In addition to the aircrew, the squadrons armourers were less than impressed, as they had to change the target indicators on each aircraft with Mallender and Gaunt expected to perform the role of 'Green marker 2' with green target indicators.

As the ground crew sweated under the evening summer sun and worked to quickly swap the target markers over, the main bomber force and Nos. 83 and 97 Squadrons started to take off at 18:45hrs (BST).

Guy Gibson and James Warwick were briefed by the experienced Controller - Squadron Leader Charles Owen before the raid, as he had acted as the Controller on the Mönchengladbach raid nine days before. In his own journal now held at the Imperial War Museum in London, Charles Owen noted that he had flown Mosquito KB213 that night and there had been, 'Few searchlights and no light flak over the target.' If Charles Owen repeated these comments in his briefing, it may have inadvertently influenced Gibson's decision about his flight-path and altitude over Holland and possibly played a part in his demise. However, Charles Owen was only trying to assist Gibson and giving an honest assessment of the target nine days before this operation.

When the author spoke with Oliver Owen in April 2024, he said his father 'admired Gibson, but could not say he liked him.' Charles Owen had written a letter to *Aeroplane Monthly* in June 1977. He stated in the letter:

> 'Guy Gibson's official appointment at Coningsby was Base Air Staff Officer. This was a staff job and he continued to fly on operations in defiance of orders to the contrary – certainly verbal and probably written – but with the very active approval of Base Commander, Air Commodore 'Bobby' Sharp…

> I briefed Gibson for his last trip as I had been Controller on the same target on September 10. His briefed route home was south-west from the target at medium height, into France and thence home. As he climbed into his aircraft, he told me that he intended to return direct from the target at low-level. I told him very forcibly what I thought of this idea, but he had made up his mind. This is unfortunately proved by the location of his final crash.'

Charles Owen had clearly reminded Gibson that their flight over occupied territory would be short and they should come back over Allied occupied France and Belgium at medium height. He also told Gibson that all aircraft were to stay above 10,000 feet until they had exited the coastline. Gibson was therefore not only planning to ignore the directives forbidding him personally from flying over enemy occupied territory for long periods of time, but he was also going against current orders for all crews regarding low-level flying over Holland and the advice of a colleague and experienced Controller. Holland was at this time a major battlefront, especially around the area of Operation Market Garden and the planners were only too aware of the number of recent low-flying flak casualties.

Guy Gibson and James Warwick started to prepare themselves for their flight. Although the pilot had flown this type of aircraft before, his navigator had to associate himself with the wireless set, and more importantly, the fuel system and the series of fuel transfer switches which would be his responsibility in the cockpit. Even though Gibson had flown a Mosquito before, his experience was quite limited with only approximately thirteen hours flying time on the type.

Robert Wilson in his article '*A warriors death*' on the website – *Australian Flight Safety* on 22 August 2022, discusses the death of Guy Gibson. Wilson states the Dutch historical author Jan van den Driesschen, claimed an engineering officer on No. 627 Squadron had to quickly describe the fuel system to James Warwick in the Mosquitos cockpit. The unnamed engineering officer adding that during his brief tutorial with Warwick, he was rudely, more or less thrown out of the cockpit by Guy Gibson. This, if correct, is similar to the time when it appears Gibson told the No. 630 Squadron flight engineer to, 'Bugger off down the back' and leave him in the Lancaster cockpit a few weeks before at East Kirkby. Clearly, on this evidence James Warwick was going to be at a distinct disadvantage and one that could have consequences for him and his pilot.

Guy Gibson clearly had a lot on his mind, he had been abrupt with his Controller colleague Charles Owen who was only trying to give him some advice, he was abrupt with Eve on the telephone; and he had reportedly *thrown* an engineering officer out of the Mosquitos cockpit. The question is why was he apparently so stressed? Could it be, Gibson suddenly realised the size of the task he was about to undertake? He had only flown as an active bomber pilot on fifteen raids in the past two years and only seven of those had been aimed at targets in Germany, including the Dams raid. He was untrained as a Pathfinder Controller and target marker and had few flying hours in the de Havilland Mosquito. He had never flown with his navigator before and that man was a complete novice on the Mosquito and its systems.

At about 19:45hrs (BST) the Mosquitos of No. 627 Squadron and that of Guy Gibson started their engines. The first to leave the ground was the aircraft of Gibson and Warwick at 19:51hrs, followed by Squadron Leader Churcher and the rest of the squadron. The last Mosquito left the ground of Woodhall Spa at 20:05hrs (BST).

As the Mosquitos headed out over the North Sea, the main bomber force and the *illuminators* from Nos. 83 and 97 Squadrons, were crossing the Belgian coast at a point between Ostend and Dunkirk. It was less than two hours to H-hour at 21:45hrs (BST).

According to Luftwaffe records, the German defences did not identify and track the main bomber force until they were near Liège, approximately 200 miles from their aiming points. The Lancasters did not climb to their bombing altitudes until they were well inside Belgium and this, together with the damage previously inflicted upon the German radar systems and their defences, allowed the force to get close to their targets before being identified. In addition, the window force (strips of foil dropped to disrupt German radar) had been very effective in misleading the Luftwaffe fighter controllers.

We know from post-war German records that the window dropping force was sighted at 21:16hrs (BST) south-east of Koblenz. They were assessed by the German controllers to be a mixed force of about sixty enemy aircraft. As a result of this information, six Messerschmitt 109G fighters of 1/NJGII were scrambled from Bonn-Hangelar and advised to undertake a *Helle Moskito Jagd* or Mosquito hunt in that area.

In addition to the Messerschmitt 109's, between 21:17 and 21:57hrs (BST) a mixed force of thirty-two Junkers 88's and Messerschmitt 110's from III/NJG1, IV/NJG1, plus the Stab and II/NJG2 were scrambled from airfields at Dortmund and Cologne Butzweilerhof. Elsewhere, Hauptmann Schmidt the Staffel Kapitan of 8/NJG1 was scrambled in his Messerschmitt 110 from Werl at 21:30hrs (BST).

It was clear the German defences had been caught off-guard and their fighter controllers only started passing information about the main raid to their pilots at about 21:43hrs (BST), just two minutes before H-hour for the bombers.

Guy Gibson and the No. 627 Squadron target markers were now inbound towards the target, while the illuminators of Nos. 83 and 97 Squadron's were in position to drop their flares and the main force was rapidly approaching. It appeared everything was going to plan for Guy Gibson.

Chapter Nine

The Mönchengladbach and Rheydt Raid

A total of 185 Avro Lancasters from Nos. 44, 49, 50, 57, 61, 101, 106, 467, 619 and 630 Squadrons were dispatched as the main force to bomb Mönchengladbach and Rheydt. In addition, Nos. 83 and 97 Squadrons sent twenty-six Lancasters to act as illuminators and ten Mosquitos from No. 627 Squadron as target markers. Not all the aircraft would arrive over Mönchengladbach and Rheydt, some aircraft returning early due to illness or technical problems, but over 200 machines would attack the twin towns.

As raid support, the Window dropping aircraft made a diversionary feint, while No. 100 Group flew a number of Serret Mosquito intruder sorties to a variety of German night-fighter airfields. This together with standard Fighter Command night-fighter patrols, aimed to minimise the risk from the German night-fighter force to the bombers.

At 21:34hrs (BST) Lancaster 'J' of No. 83 Squadron arrived over the target area of Mönchengladbach. The pilot, Flying Officer Gamble and his crew dropped their flares to illuminate the target from 15,500 feet, but would later report seeing no sign of any target marking by the Mosquitos of No. 627 Squadron. The red target indicators should have been the first markers to be dropped, but there was no sign of them.

At 21:35hrs, Lancasters 'F' and 'L' of No. 83 Squadron dropped their flares, but the Lancaster crews could not see any red target indicators, just green and yellow TIs. Flight Lieutenant Jennings in Lancaster 'A' later told the intelligence officers at his debriefing that they dropped their illumination flares, but no target markers were seen, even though they heard a Mosquito pilot shout 'Tally-ho' over the radio at 21:38hrs. A few minutes later, they saw green TIs to the north-east of the target. (The tally-ho call was probably that of Flight Lieutenant Bartlett in Green marker 1.)

Squadron Leader Hatcher in Lancaster 'L' of No. 83 Squadron reported dropping his illumination flares, but again no red TIs were observed. Eventually, he saw the green and yellow TIs, but Hatcher reported it was difficult to hear the Controller over the radio and the VHF signal was very weak.

The other illuminating squadron – No. 97, arrived over the target at a similar time to No. 83 Squadron. Various crews reported dropping their flares and noting the target area was well illuminated, but there was no sign of the red target markers.

Australian, Flight Lieutenant Schofield, in No. 97 Squadron Lancaster 'O' for Orange, reported dropping his flares as ordered by the Controller. He said the Controller reported his flares were excellent and the town was very well illuminated, but still no red target markers were observed.

The crew of 'F' for Freddie dropped their illumination flares and as they left the target area their rear gunner reported seeing a single red target indicator behind them.

In 1993, the *Grantham Journal* published a supplement called *Dambusters Remembered.* Contained within the supplement were a large number of reminiscences about the Dambusters and Guy Gibson. On page 38 there was a story titled *Last glimpse of plane.* The story detailed the sighting of Gibson that night by Flying Officer John Humphreys, a flight engineer with No. 97 Squadron, although the report said he was a bomb aimer.

Over Rheydt, John Humphreys said he could see two Mosquitos below their Lancaster. Gibson flew in to drop a red marker on the aiming point, but he couldn't release it and Humphreys says he heard him call out instructions to the other Mosquito on the R/T. The other pilot could not identify the aiming point, so Gibson could be heard telling him, 'Follow me in, when I reach the aiming point, I'll flash my navigation lights so you can drop the marker.' John Humphreys believes the marker was dropped and he saw Gibson flashing his navigation lights.

Humphreys told the journalist that he believed Gibson was laying himself wide open to a fighter attack and flak, but he was determined to get the best results. That was the last time he saw the Mosquito.

If this account is correct and there is no reason to doubt it, it would not be the first time Gibson had flashed his navigation lights at low-level over a target. Gibson had flown back and forth over the Möhne Dam flashing his lights to distract the enemy gunners, while the other Lancasters carried out their attacks on the target. Gibson would have known he was making himself a target for the anti-aircraft gunners and any fighter pilot in the vicinity, however, as we shall see, a number of Lancasters also had their navigation lights on that night.

The intelligence debriefing of Nos. 83 and 97 Squadrons crews clearly indicated that there were problems with the red target indicators and radio communication with the Controller (Guy Gibson).

Flying Officer Coulter of No. 97 Squadron reported being over the target at Mönchengladbach at 21:37hrs (BST), but owing to a misunderstanding, they did not drop their flares. At 21:44hrs, they heard a call from the Controller for more illumination flares to be dropped, so they orbited and were preparing to release their flares, when the Controller gave an order for the main bomber force to bomb the target. Coulter therefore instructed his bomb aimer to release their bombs and not their flares.

Perhaps one of the best post raid debriefings came from No. 97 Squadron's Flight Lieutenant Parker. He reported seeing no target indicators before or after they dropped their bombs. They dropped their own flares over the target which was well illuminated, before passing on instructions from the Controller for more flares at 21:43hrs (BST). Two minutes later, the Controller ordered all bombing to stop and all aircraft to standby. At 21:54hrs, the Controller ordered the bombers to bomb the green TIs and for all aircraft to return to base at 21:57hrs. The crew's final debriefing comment was the 'Marking was unsatisfactory.'

Fellow No. 97 Squadron pilot, Flying Officer Negus and his crew dropped their flares at 21:48hrs (BST). They reportedly heard the Controller asking for more flares on the VHF radio and their flight engineer spotted a single red TI on the south side of the flares. At 21:52hrs, their wireless operator received an order from the Controller to 'Attack green TI direct.' The same order was not heard on the VHF system and no green TI was observed by the crew.

New Zealand Squadron Leader S.M. Smith and his crew reported seeing the first flares falling at 21:35 and 21:40hrs (BST). They then heard Marker 1 (believed to be Red marker 1 – Squadron Leader Churcher) say he was going in. At 21:42hrs Smith's crew heard the Controller say he could see everything and the illumination flares were good.

Smith and his crew claimed the Controller made a run over the Rheydt aiming point, but his target indicator hung-up. After this, they heard the other target marking Mosquitos say they could not identify the aiming point and suggested more flares should be dropped. At 21:43hrs more flares were called for by the Controller and at 21:45hrs the red bombing force (i.e. aircraft briefed to strike the red target markers) was told to stand-by by the Controller.

Squadron Leader Smith and his crew claimed no red markers had been dropped by 21:49hrs, so the Controller ordered the force to bomb the green TIs (in Mönchengladbach). At that moment, 'Red marker 1' dropped a TI on his aiming point (the rail yards at Rheydt), so the Controller changed his orders back to bombing the red TI with an overshoot. Once this was completed, Smith and his crew heard Gibson order all aircraft to return to base and congratulated the flare force for their fine efforts.

This detailed account from Squadron Leader Smith was corroborated by two other No. 97 Squadron crews, those of Flying Officer Ryan and Flight Lieutenant Brooker.

Flying Officer Geoff King was a bomb-aimer on Flight Lieutenant Laing's crew in Lancaster PB401 of No. 97 Squadron that night. He gave an audio statement to the Imperial War Museum many decades after the event. He recalled:

> 'Gibson was our Master bomber and he came to lunch with us in the Mess prior to briefing. From my own point of view, it was not a very successful raid, because my H2S started to play up from our flare release point and the only thing we could do was to back up those already over the target. We heard Gibson's instructions – they were very plain and to the point.'

The two Pathfinder Lancaster squadrons deputed to drop the illumination flares, had witnessed something of a nightmare as far as Gibson's controlling baptism was concerned. The VHF communications were poor and his backup W/T system was also intermittent, but the main issue came from the Mosquito marker force. Considering the fractured relationship between No. 627 Squadron and Gibson was not the most amiable, it would be easy to think this might have been caused in some way by animosity, but it wasn't.

Red marker 1 and Deputy Controller was Squadron Leader Churcher and his navigator Pilot Officer Willis. En route to the target, an exhaust stub on their port Rolls-Royce Merlin engine came loose and Churcher had to feather the propellors. This caused them to drop back from the main formation and delayed their arrival over the target area. Wanting to complete their target marking task, Churcher restarted the engine to speed up and arrived over the target at 21:40hrs (BST). Unfortunately, as they arrived on the approach to the target, the loose exhaust stub flew off and the glare from the engine, made it impossible for him to see over the port side of the aircraft, while hindering the crew's night vision.

Squadron Leader Ron Churcher made an attempt to mark the red aiming point, but he could not see the aiming point due to the glare from his damaged engine. This caused the delay in marking the red aiming point over Rheydt, while sowing confusion among the main bomber force and undoubtedly Guy Gibson. Gibson now decided to take control like any good leader. He could see the red aiming point at Rheydt in the light of the flares and tried to drop his own red TI on the aiming point. Unfortunately, his red target indicator hung-up and did not leave the bomb bay of his Mosquito. Unable to mark the target, Gibson flew across the target flashing his navigation lights and calling out to the other Mosquitos, but the other red markers could not see him. Gibson therefore requested that more flares be dropped to assist the Mosquito crews in locating the red aiming point.

Eventually, Ron Churcher was able to mark the aiming point with a single red TI at 21:50hrs (BST), but it was late and had already caused considerable delay and confusion to the main bomber force.

Red marker 2 (Flight Lieutenants Hanlon and Tice) arrived over the target at 21:33hrs (BST), but did not mark the red aiming point as they could not locate it. Red marker 3 (Flying Officer Brown and Flight Lieutenant Cowan) followed Ron Churcher in, all be it late, due to their leader's problems. After Churcher's single red TI had been dropped, they dropped their own red TIs on top of it at about 21:51hrs. As soon as the target was suitably marked, all be it late, Gibson told the red marking aircraft to go home.

Guy Gibson, as the Controller, had tried to recover the situation, bringing a temporary pause to the bombing and telling the orbiting bombers to aim for the green TIs. When Churcher suddenly dropped his red TI, which was followed up by Red marker 3 at about 21:51hrs, Gibson directed the remaining red main force aircraft to revert to the red TI aiming point. Although there was some confusion, Guy Gibson had managed a difficult situation and prevented a total failure.

Over Mönchengladbach, Green marker 1 (Flight Lieutenants Bartlett and Mitchell) dived from 2,000 feet to 700 feet, marking their target with a green TI at 21:37hrs (BST). Their target marker went through the roof of the target and was partially obscured, but Green 2 and Green 3 backed up this marker over the next couple of minutes and the main force arrived to drop their bombs on the green TIs at 21:43hrs (BST).

Green marker 2 was crewed by Flight Lieutenants Mallender and Gaunt in Mosquito KB213, the aircraft discarded by Gibson at Woodhall Spa. They had no problems with the aircraft or their target marking that night and would return home safely.

The Yellow marker flight, which included Ken Oatley and his pilot Jock Walker, who Gibson had punished following the fracas in No. 627 Squadron's Officers' Mess, successfully marked their aiming point in the railway marshalling yards in north-eastern Mönchengladbach between 21:39 and 21:43hrs (BST).

Yellow marker 3 (Flying Officer Whitehead and Pilot Officer Watt) suffered a hung-up yellow target indicator like Gibson. It is unclear whether they brought it back to Woodhall Spa or dropped it and the bomb cradle over the North Sea as per standard operating policy.

The main bomber force arrived over the three aiming points at or after 21:40hrs (BST). No. 44 Squadron was the first to arrive and bombed the green TIs, nineteen of their aircraft being briefed to attack Mönchengladbach. They reported the target area to be hazy and hard to locate, with the green TIs not being very bright and the red TIs north and not south of the green TIs. A number of their crews reported the VHF radio to be poor and the Controller's orders were not clearly received. This made it difficult to pass on any instructions to other aircraft. One No. 44 Squadron crew reported there being few searchlights and little light flak, while another saw fighter flares (flares dropped to enable night-fighters to see the bombers). One crew also claimed the trip was very unpleasant due to an electrical storm encountered over Holland on the way home.

No. 207 Squadron's eighteen aircraft also attacked Mönchengladbach. One crew commanded by Flying Officer Wells reportedly heard Gibson telling the Deputy Controller (Ron Churcher) that the flares had fallen in open countryside. The Controller ordered the squadron to bomb the yellow target indicators. Several No. 207 Squadron crews also reported a storm on the return journey across Holland and one crew reported many aircraft flying with their navigation lights on. One aircraft reportedly had its lights on twenty miles from the Dutch coastline, while another crew reported sighting an enemy night-fighter with its navigation lights illuminated.

No. 467 Squadron (RAAF) sent nineteen aircraft to Rheydt and there was some confusion in their debriefing reports when they returned home.

One crew specifically reported that the target marking was not thought to be of recent attack standards, while other crews reported that the aiming point was not marked, aircraft had dropped their bombs before being given permission and Squadron Leader Deignan reported, 'Controlling and marking left much to be desired.'

Flying Officer Mayes heard the Controller say, 'Come in and bomb,' but he did not hear him say bomb anything in particular.

Another crew heard the Controller say bomb the green spot (TI) but they could not see a green target indicator. One crew were on their run-in to bomb a green TI as ordered, when the Controller suddenly told them to change to the Red TI as originally briefed. It was clear the Australians crews were less than impressed that night!

No. 630 Squadron sent seventeen aircraft to Mönchengladbach and sixteen of them attacked the target. They were ordered to bomb the yellow TIs and encountered a few enemy night-fighters, but these air-to-air combats were inconclusive.

No. 619 Squadron's sixteen aircraft bombed Mönchengladbach, some of them bombing the green target indicators, but others dropped their bombs on the fires as they could not see the green TIs.

Guy Gibson's old unit, No. 106 Squadron, sent eighteen Lancasters to bomb Rheydt. Their commanding officer, Wing Commander Stevens, reported the red TIs as being too late. He therefore bombed the green TIs as directed by the Controller, but the attack was late at 21:54hrs (BST) and he considered the raid to have been very poor. Other No. 106 Squadron crews similarly changed to bomb the green TIs as ordered by Gibson, but the odd crew who bombed around 21:55hrs struck the late red target indictor.

Nos. 61 and 101 Squadrons had also been tasked with bombing Rheydt with twenty aircraft. They, like No. 106 Squadron, had to bomb the green TIs as the red indicators were late. No. 101 Squadron had some of the last aircraft over the target, one aircraft bombing the red TIs at 21:57hrs (BST).

No. 57 Squadron tasked seventeen aircraft with attacking Mönchengladbach. The squadron reported the marking to have been accurate and punctual, but sadly their Operations Record Book and other records do not give details of their times over the target or individual crew comments.

No. 50 Squadron's nineteen aircraft visited Rheydt between 21:53 and 21:57hrs (BST) and again, they reported the target marking to be confusing. Flying Officer Amey attacked at 21:53hrs and bombed the green TIs as instructed by the Controller. He recalled clearly hearing the Controller telling other aircraft to wait and stand-by, as number one marker (Churcher) could not drop his target indicator. The Controller then told aircraft to bomb the green TI, just before a red TI was finally observed.

Flying Officer Marris attacked at 21:54hrs (BST) and saw both the red and green TIs, he therefore bombed the red marker as initially briefed. Marris also reported seeing two aircraft leaving the target area with their navigation lights on. Various other crews from this unit also reported seeing bombers with their navigation lights on and Flying Officer Sweetman stated, 'I think it unnecessary for aircraft to keep navigation lights on until nearing the front line.'

Sergeant Arthur Emlyn Williams, the mid-upper gunner in Flying Officer Farrar's crew (No. 50 Squadron Lancaster

LM236), later recalled in an audio statement to the International Bomber Command Centre in Lincoln:

> 'It's possible that I am the only remaining crew member to hear his voice over the intercom (Guy Gibson). These were his words of course, "Hello main force. This is your master leader calling. I am down at two thousand feet. I can see everything bang on."'

Arthur Williams added, 'We were at a height of eleven thousand feet above Rheydt. Gibson did not survive that operation and there are several rumours as to his death.' Sadly, Arthur did not expand upon what these rumours were, but they are probably similar to those discussed later in this book.

Finally, No. 49 Squadron sent twelve aircraft to Mönchengladbach and bombed between 21:46 and 21:54hrs (BST). The crews reported the target marking to be inadequate and the target indicators were obscured. Although there were concerns about the target marking, Squadron Leader Gorton reported that the 'Controller directed well'; while Group Captain Weir, who flew with the squadron that night, later reported there to have been no flak or fighters.

The raid officially concluded at 21:58hrs (BST). Guy Gibson was still orbiting the target area and probably assessing the results of the bombing at about 22:00hrs. Like any Controller, he would ensure the area was clear and the bombers were on their way home before he left the target.

When he left the target area, Gibson appears to have still had his full complement of target indicators in his Mosquitos bomb bay, including the hung-up red TI which failed to drop some twenty minutes before the conclusion of the raid.

Guy Gibson's last known radio communication was around the time the raid concluded, as he circled the twin towns. What happened to him after that would become something of a mystery.

The main force of Lancasters headed westwards from Germany, crossing the Dutch border within a few minutes and passing to the south of Eindhoven and the main area of Operation Market Garden. Their course took them south of the ground fighting and near Turnhout in Belgium, the bomber stream which remained at about 10,000 feet, turned onto a north-westerly heading. The formation eventually crossed the Dutch coastline over the various islands to the south of Rotterdam and headed back over the North Sea to England.

It is believed Gibson decided to disregard orders and advice and remained at low-level, taking a direct route across the German border into Holland. It appears he ignored his friend Charles Owen and was in a hurry to get home.

From the German border he is believed to have taken a direct route over the vicinity of the recently liberated town of Eindhoven, a large conurbation which was still surrounded by elements of the German army and the Waffen-SS. The area bristled with anti-aircraft guns, especially the fearsome 20mm low-level flak guns. Gibson's homeward route appears to have passed over, or very close to, the heavily defended Luftwaffe night-fighter base at Gilze-Rijen, an airfield where No. 617 Squadron's Pilot Officer Lewis Burpee and his crew had died on the Dams raid in May 1943.

What happened to Guy Gibson in the thirty minutes after he left the target area is a mystery and one that has been discussed for decades, but ultimately it resulted in his death at Steenbergen in Holland.

Chapter Ten

Mosquito Down

At approximately 22:30hrs (BST) the inhabitants of Steenbergen, a small Dutch town about half way between Antwerp and Rotterdam, heard the approach of a low-flying aircraft. For the past half hour, the residents had been kept awake in their darkened homes, listening as the Lancaster bombers of No. 5 Group headed home to England. The droning of British night bombers was nothing new to the people of this small town, but now they heard something different, something which sounded unusual.

Mr. S. Bastiannse was sitting with his wife in their home in Blauwstraat, a street that runs more or less in a north to south direction, south of the town's large gothic church. Suddenly, the couple heard an aircraft with spluttering engines approaching their home and they hurried out into their rear garden, just in time to see the aircraft approaching from the east of the town.

Mr. Bastiannse later estimated the aircraft's altitude to have been no more than 3,500 feet (he originally gave this height in metres) and the couple could clearly see the crew in the cockpit, illuminated by what Bastiannse called a bright light inside the aircraft. As the aircraft passed by, there was a sudden large explosion and the machine fell to the ground to the west of the town centre.

The Van der Riet farm stood on the West Graaf Hendrik Polder to the north-west of the town centre, surrounded by farm land and dikes. A few hundred yards away on the edge of the town, was a small sugar factory and the noise of the aircraft attracted the attention of the night watchman – Anton de Bruyn. He would later report, that he heard what he thought was an aircraft circling the town and went outside to take a look. Looking skywards he saw the aircraft and noticed, like Mr. Bastiannse and his wife, that the cockpit interior was emitting a bright light, in which the crewmen could clearly be discerned. The aircrafts engines then spluttered and a trail of flames and sparks trailed back behind the machine as it dived into the open ground between the factory and the Van der Riet farmhouse. As it hit the farmland it exploded in a vivid flash, leaving some burning wreckage on the surface.

Anton de Bruyn did not identify from which engine the flames originated or whether both of the aircraft's engines were on fire.

In the farmhouse, the Van der Riet family were asleep, but their two sons, 14-year-old Frans and 16-year-old Jan, heard the approaching aircraft which they recalled made an odd whistling sound before it crashed and exploded. Quickly grabbing their coats, the two teenage boys made their way outside to find a fire blazing in the middle of the field adjacent to the farm. It was about 100-200 metres from their farmhouse, although a low mist hung over the field which prevented them having a clear view of the site.

The two brothers and their father, who had also risen, later described the blaze as giving off a reddish glow, but the flames soon died down and they thought it could have been a stray bomb, rather than an aircraft, so they returned to bed. The boys' father, fearful of the German curfew, had decided to stay inside the farmhouse until morning and did not venture outside, watching the scene from a window.

Jan Van Oers, a blacksmith, also lived on the Van der Riet farm and he observed the aircraft from an attic window. He thought the aircraft was travelling south to north and was burning and giving off a whistling sound before it crashed. Van Oers went outside and up on to Haven-dijk. where he met a local man called Albert Van der Werf. The two men walked towards the blazing wreckage which they now described as having a bluish flame. Thinking there was nothing they could do the two men went home as the flames started to die down.

Whether the Mosquito had been circling the town before the crash is unclear, but the perception of some of the witnesses, was that is what had occurred. Little did anyone in the town realise at the time, but the leader of the Dambusters – Guy Gibson VC and his navigator James Warwick had crashed to their deaths on that small plot of farm land.

Over the years, there has been speculation about whether the reddish glow in the fire could have been caused by Gibson's hung-up red target indicator; while the bluish flame was more likely due to a burning metal alloy or a possibly a combination of the different coloured TIs.

The whistling noise could have come from the engines or even holes in the wooden wings and fuselage, the air passing over them and creating the sound like some odd form of a woodwind musical instrument. If there were holes in the aircrafts structure, could this damage have been caused by enemy flak?

The Mosquitos of No. 627 Squadron all returned safely home to Woodhall Spa, all that is, apart from that flown by Guy Gibson and James Warwick. The aircrews went to their standard debriefing and the intelligence officers discussed the raid which was deemed to have been somewhat confused, exacerbated by Ron Churcher's loose exhaust stub and the poor radio communications.

Although Gibson and Warwick were not present, most of the Mosquito crews thought they had landed at Coningsby and had not wished to take part in No. 627 Squadron's intelligence debriefing. (This would not have been surprising considering the simmering relations between Gibson and the squadron personnel.)

Later, after many of the crews had gone off to bed or to the Officers' Mess for a late drink, a telephone call was received from Coningsby Operations, asking if Gibson had landed at Woodhall Spa. When it was realised he had not landed at Coningsby or Woodhall Spa, there was a perceived possibility he had landed elsewhere, especially as the expected fog had started to come down over Lincolnshire. Further telephone calls were made, but the further enquiries revealed this to be incorrect and Gibson could not be located. Gibson and Warwick were posted as missing and calls were made to Group and Bomber Command Headquarters to give them the bad news.

The following morning, Mr. Van der Riet went out to start work on his farm. He went to his tool shed and was shocked to find a limbless torso propped up against the wall of the building, the head limply hanging down to one side. In a state of shock, he quickly ran back into the farmhouse to warn his wife and teenage boys of his gruesome find. The farmer quickly decided to inform the local Chief of Police in Steenbergen of his find, this was a man called Van der Kassteele and he in turn, informed the local German commander.

The Germans authorities quickly dispatched soldiers to the area of the farm and the adjacent crash site, blocking roads to all inquisitive civilians. There was not much of the aircraft left to see, just an engine, a main wheel and some fragments visible on the surface. Other larger items had buried themselves deep into the earth or been obliterated in the fire.

Two Dutch auxiliary policemen named Stofellen and Van Mechelen attended the site where they found about twelve soldiers, the local German commander and a German Chaplain – Oberleutnant Blok. The two Dutchmen asked if they could search for human remains, but the commander told them 'Terror Fliegers' did not deserve a burial. Van Mechelen immediately challenged the German commander with the fact the British had given Baron von Richthofen a full military funeral in 1918, and with the support of the German chaplain, permission was eventually given to search for any human remains.

The torso and head found at the wall of the farm building were carefully placed into a basket. The dog tags around the neck of the torso and head bore the name J.B. Warwick and his service number 156612. Van Mechelen removed the dog tags and placed them into his own pocket, without telling the Germans of his find.

The search continued and the two policemen soon found two arms, two lower legs with feet – still inside their burnt shoes, before finding a third foot indicating the presence of two sets of remains. A piece of skull was soon located and a severed hand. The hand reportedly had a gold ring on one of its fingers, which was also removed and hidden from the German authorities. The ring had Warwick's initials J.B.W. inscribed upon it.

Eventually, the personal items were handed over to the Dutch Chief of Police and the human remains were taken to the town's mortuary in Blauwstraat, the same street in which Mr. and Mrs. Bastiannse resided.

Amongst the other personal effects found was a booklet on fishing and an envelope addressed to *S/Ldr. J.B. Warwick DFC, RAF Station Coningsby, Lincoln.* The carrying of such a document on an operational sortie was against all Air Ministry directives and it may be indicative that James Warwick had no intention of flying that day before Guy Gibson press-ganged and designated him as his navigator.

Other items included a single black service tie, an Omega watch, a forage cap, a piece of uniform, a button, the travelling aircraft servicing form and a number of maps. An escape kit containing a number of French, Dutch and Belgian bank notes was also located at the crash site.

The German personnel at the scene had no idea of the actual identity of the two victims, although the Dutch Chief of Police had the name Squadron Leader James Warwick on some of the personal items they had recovered. Collectively, both the

Germans and the Dutch were oblivious to the fact they had the remains of a famous, highly decorated RAF pilot in their midst.

Initially a small coffin was made by a local carpenter and all the remains were placed inside it. A brass plate was inscribed with the name J.B. Warwick and an unknown soldier, before being screwed onto the coffin lid.

A short time later, some of the local children were seen playing with 'something' near the crash site, some accounts saying this was in a hedgerow. The object was found to be the remains of a sock, with a laundry tag bearing the name Gibson attached to it. This was clearly the name of the second man and the name plate was removed from the coffin lid and turned over. It was then inscribed with the names J.B. Warwick and Gibson.

The local Dutch community had wanted to give the two airmen an honourable funeral, with their air raid wardens as pall bearers. They also wanted to drape the single coffin with the Dutch flag, but German officials refused to sanction this event, fearing a demonstration with the Allied forces advancing across Holland. The German commander therefore ordered the funeral to take place immediately and without fanfare.

Despite the German commander's orders, the coffin was draped in the Dutch flag and the small cortege with a horse-drawn hearse made its way to the Roman Catholic cemetery at the south end of the town where a small impromptu crowd had gathered.

The local Mayor Chris Herbers and the Town Clerk J.L. Jurgens led the few mourners that were allowed to attend and the ceremony was conducted by a Roman Catholic priest – Father Verhoeven and the Lutheran Pastor – Van den Brink.

The Lutheran Pastor recited the Lord's Prayer in English and when the funeral was concluded, the local grave digger quickly filled in the grave and the crowd dispersed.

A short time later, a simple white wooden cross with the names *Squadron Leader J.B. Warwick DFC and Gibson RAF* was placed at the head of the grave. It also bore the date of the crash.

In London on the afternoon of 20 September, Eve Gibson received the dreaded telegram, telling her that Guy was reported missing on an operational flight on the night of the 19/20 September. Like many before her, Eve later recalled being numb with shock and she sat for some time as the information sunk in.

There was a national media blackout in relation to Guy Gibson being posted as missing, this was partly to avoid informing the Germans who they had in captivity if he had been captured, or who they had killed. However, news soon started to leak out and Flight Lieutenant Ron Williams, in a letter home to his parents on 26 September 1944, from Woodhall Spa noted:

> 'It has not been announced yet, but Guy Gibson went for a burton in a Mosquito over the Ruhr a week ago. The Germans will have a good time if they get hold of him!'

At Woodhall Spa, the loss of Guy Gibson was met with some indifference. Many of the No. 627 Squadron crews disliked Guy Gibson and his loss was no surprise to them. He was perceived as egotistical and bumptious, while he was untrained and unqualified to undertake the role of a Controller. There was some sympathy for his navigator James Warwick, a man who was also untrained for his role with no experience of Mosquitos, but most people assumed he had been ordered to go on this mission.

All Mosquito crewmen knew the aircraft required a close bond and teamwork to operate it to its full potential, especially in the marking and controlling roles. Gibson and Warwick were not specifically trained on this type of aircraft, the pilot having at most, just thirteen hours flying time on the Mosquito, while Warwick had never flown in one. Neither man was trained for target marking or Controller duties.

In many respects, the fact Gibson thought he could turn-up and undertake the duties of a Controller without any thorough training or experience, was perceived by many as being arrogant and typical of the man. He was undoubtedly a skilled and experienced pilot, but this was a very different type of flying when compared to his previous experiences. The assumption he could just turn up and take on a role, a role which took the No. 627 Squadron crews many days and weeks of training to perfect, did not endear him to that unit's personnel.

Sergeant and later Warrant Officer Harry Parkins from No. 630 Squadron still did not like Gibson. He said he never liked the man and told another airman about his own previous experience with Gibson. The airman responded by telling Harry, 'You're not the first one to say that, there was a young pilot who was just about to take off, walking up to his plane and Guy Gibson happened to be there. He called the young pilot over and said, "Don't you ever salute your superiors?"

The young pilot said he didn't know you still saluted when on operations, but Gibson was angry and told the pilot he would be reduced in rank when he returned. The pilot officer was reduced to the rank of Sergeant."'

In September 1944, Harry Parkins came back off an operation and went into a pub. 'All of a sudden there was a shout, with everybody saying "Wahey."' Harry asked if the war had finished? and was told by one airman, 'No, Guy Gibson's caught the bucket.' Harry added – 'Guy Gibson was not popular.'

This was not the only occasion Guy Gibson demanded a salute or respect. Alex Kinnear, from No. 106 Squadron, recalled the time his crew went for a night out. As their vehicle passed a Hillman pick-up truck outside the Station Headquarters at Coningsby, they noticed an RAF officer trying to crank start the vehicle. Alex's crew shouted in unison as they drove past the vehicle, 'Swing it chum,' unaware that Gibson was in the truck. Next morning, Gibson had Alex Kinnear and his crew lined up in front of him and he tore into them. He said discipline was getting slack and that from that time onwards, all NCO's would salute all officers. Alex said Gibson occasionally took stands like that.

What had happened to Gibson was a mystery and decades later, no one knows what had happened to him that night. Various hypotheses have been discussed, some of which were impossible.

Harry Parkins states in his audio statement, now at the International Bomber Command Centre, that he thought Gibson was flying a Mosquito, and on his way home from the target. Instead of keeping with the others, he spotted a train and decided to go down and shoot this train up. He was hit by rifle fire in a fuel tank and blew up, but the story was hushed up he added. Another account, according to Harry, was that Gibson was brought down by flak.

We know Gibson's Mosquito did not have guns or cannon, so an attack upon a train was impossible, but it is clear there were various stories and rumours circulating at the time. No one knew exactly what had happened to him.

How Air Marshal Harris, Cochrane and Sharp felt upon receipt of the news that Gibson was missing is unknown. Harris and Cochrane did make some later comments, as did the Prime Minister once it was formally announced that Gibson was missing believed killed; but there was a media blackout and apart from the gossip among the airmen, very little was said.

On 4 November 1944, the Allied army liberated Steenbergen and a Canadian officer took statements from a number of witnesses to the crash. He was given what few personal effects had been salvaged from the crash site, including James Warwick's dog tags. The information was relayed back to London and the Air Ministry and on 19 November, Air Marshal Arthur Harris sent a telegram to the Officers' Mess and No. 617 Squadron at Woodhall Spa. It stated:

> 'Regret to inform the Mess that W/C Gibson G.P. and S/L Warwick J.B. now confirmed killed as a result of air operations over Germany on night of 19 Sept. I have informed the Prime Minister and NoK. Harris, Air Marshal.'

Guy Gibson and James Warwick were eventually publicly listed as missing on 29 November 1944. The following day, the nation's media reported that Guy Gibson was missing on operations, but many airmen were reported as missing, only to turn up later, either in hospital or in a prisoner of war camp. However, deep down most people must have feared the worst, while some knew there was already a grave in Steenbergen.

The Air Ministry media release was somewhat misleading, but it was repeated by various newspaper outlets across Britain, the Commonwealth, and the United States where Gibson had been so warmly received just a year before.

The *Daily Mail* headline stated: 'Wingco Guy Gibson, Dam VC Missing after "Master" raid.'

The *Birmingham Daily Gazette* headline stated: 'Guy Gibson VC is Missing – Hero of the great attack on the Möhne and Eder dams.' The account then explained that, 'As a master bomber, Gibson's experience was of great assistance in perfecting this comparatively new technique.'

It is clear that the Air Ministry and the protocols of propaganda, meant that rather than being seen as a novice Controller, the great missing dambuster was assisting through his great experience, in perfecting the relatively new technique of target marking.

The *Western Morning News* went further stating:

> 'Gibson, hero of the Möhne Dam attack was flying that night as a Master bomber, much lower than the main force. At a quarter to ten, he was heard over the target giving unhurried instructions in his usual calm voice. He finished his job and was not heard of again.'

Guy Gibson, who was already a hero to the British public, was elevated even further by these newspaper stories. The fact the accounts were not exactly correct in terms of the mission and his assistance in developing target marking and controlling, was not an issue when propaganda was at work.

Although the Allies had liberated Steenbergen in early November 1944, no investigation was undertaken to identify the cause of the crash. Why should Guy Gibson's fatal crash be investigated, when so many others were not? Sadly, he was one of many airmen killed on operations over Europe. The fact is he had been killed and as far as the authorities were concerned, he lay with James Warwick in a joint grave in the town's Roman Catholic cemetery. What did it matter how Guy Gibson and his navigator had died? The war was still in full swing across Europe and the Far East and many more would die before peace resumed.

When exactly Eve was told of the location of her husband's body is not clear, but the family solicitors who dealt with Gibson's will made a statement that his body had been located and the media were once again quick to pick up the story, such was the aurora that still surrounded the great Dambuster.

On 31 January 1945, the *Daily Mail*, the *Daily Mirror* and the *Birmingham Mail* along with other newspapers, reported that Guy Gibson's body had now been found. The *Birmingham Mail* reported that the widow of Guy Gibson VC, known as 'The Dambuster', has received official notification that his body has been located. His aurora was further enhanced when their story continued:

> 'He was one of the most brilliant pilots Bomber Command has ever had, said an Air Ministry tribute. He had a natural easy manner, which made him loved by the crews under him.'

Guy Gibson was, by the end of the war, one of the nation's greatest heroes, he was fondly remembered and no one would speak ill of the dead hero. Although some of the tributes that followed, not to mention Richard Todd's portrayal of him in the Dambusters movie conflict with some of the evidence in this book, he was still a very highly regarded individual. He was a skilled pilot, a brave leader and a man determined to do his duty.

The question was, what had brought him down on the night of 19 September 1944? In the next chapter, we shall examine the various hypotheses.

Chapter Eleven

What Could Have Happened?

There are a number of reasons why Guy Gibson's Mosquito could have crashed that night in Steenbergen and the most obvious is enemy action via flak or a night-fighter. Therefore, we must examine the flak and night-fighter defences over Holland and Western Germany that night and in the days leading up to 19 September 1944.

As already discussed, the very experienced Squadron Leader Charles Owen, a man who was just twenty-one years of age, had flown as the Controller on the raid to Mönchengladbach, nine days prior to Gibson's final mission. According to his own journal, held in the Imperial War Museum, he found the target to be lightly defended with few searchlights and no light flak. He added that he got a good view of the target from 4,000 feet. This information was almost certainly passed on to Gibson when Owen gave him a pre-flight briefing on the afternoon of 19 September, but the situation was fluid and quite dynamic across Holland and the Ruhr Valley at this time.

With the retreat of the German army, a number of anti-aircraft forces had regrouped and consolidated both in Holland and over the border in Western Germany. In addition, elements of the 9th & 10th SS Panzer divisions had been redeployed around Arnhem to rest and re-equip. These SS divisions had their own light flak units, which were spread out across the likely flight path of Guy Gibson on his return journey, but their exact number is hard to confirm.

Although it is difficult to be precise on the number of flak guns along the probable flight path of Gibson, the number of aircraft shot down in the area over the preceding forty-eight hours was very high and indicative of a heavy concentration of flak guns. Some commentators have stated that during the course of Operation Market Garden, the Allies lost sixty-eight large aircraft (such as Dakotas and Short Stirling glider tugs), seventy-one gliders and twenty single seat fighters. There were even reports that SS units employed their 20mm flak guns against the paratroopers as they floated down to earth. If this was correct, we can assume there were a considerable number of these guns in the area.

On the night of 17-18 September, forty-eight Mosquitos from No. 8 Group's Light Night Striking Force, crossed Holland to attack Dortmund and Bremen, they were backed up by others on diversionary and countermeasure sorties. In addition, there were twenty-nine Mosquito night-fighter patrols. Although no Mosquitos were lost that night, six aircraft returned with varying degrees of flak damage.

Only four days after Gibson's loss, Charles Owen acted as Controller on a No. 5 Group raid to the Dortmund-Ems Canal. This time he noted in his journal, that they, 'met trouble over Arnhem,' giving an indication of the hot reception any aircraft would receive in the area of Operation Market Garden. In addition, he also stated that there was, 'bags of flak and searchlights' over Essen, about twenty-five miles north-east of Mönchengladbach.

Guy Gibson's likely direct flight path passed either over or close to the Luftwaffe base at Gilze-Rijen between Tilburg and Breda. This airfield, although close to the front line, was still active and was not liberated until the end of October 1944. Like all Luftwaffe airfields, it bristled with flak guns, especially the deadly 20mm variety, which was often mounted in groups of four. These 20mm guns were deadly against low-flying aircraft and aircraft attacking any airfield would undertake a variety of 'jinking' manoeuvres to avoid the flak. If a lone Mosquito flew over in a straight line, it would have been easy prey for the gunners. The flak gunners would have been aware of the returning main bomber stream crossing Holland, so they would have been on stand-by and could easily have accounted for Gibson's Mosquito.

RAF Intelligence records show a number of British aircraft failed to return that night, as well as that flown by Gibson and Warwick.

No. 106 Squadron lost Lancaster PB359 (ZN-T) with three of the crew being killed and the remainder captured. The aircraft was hit over Rheydt and crashed near a church in Rheydt-Giesenkirchen at 21:52hrs (BST). Three German night-fighters crews made claims for a Lancaster at this time and location, as did a single flak unit.

Hauptmann Hermann Greiner 11/NJG1 claimed a Lancaster at an altitude of 2,800 metres west-south-west of Mönchengladbach at 21:55hrs (BST), while Feldwebel Wilhelm Jansen of Stab 1/NJG11 claimed a probable victory at 21:53hrs (BST) at 3,500 metres near Mönchengladbach. Finally, Feldwebel Erwin Egeler of Stab IV/NJG1, claimed an aircraft at an altitude of 2,600 meters west-south-west of Mönchengladbach at 21:58hrs (BST).

A second No. 106 Squadron Lancaster, PB347, was lost with six of the crew killed and the seventh a prisoner of war. The aircraft came down at 22:15hrs (BST) near Elmpt, a town about fifteen miles west-north-west of Mönchengladbach. The aircraft may have been that claimed by Oberleutnant Fritz Lau of 4/NJG1, he claimed a Lancaster at this time and twenty-five miles west-north-west of Mönchengladbach while flying a Messerschmitt 110.

No. 467 Squadron lost Lancaster PB299 (PO-O) at 22:10hrs (BST) south-west of Eindhoven, four of the crew being killing. One of the crew, Flight Sergeant Larkin, later reported that they had been shot down by an enemy night-fighter at about 11,000 feet. The Lancasters demise has often been attributed to Leutnant Friederich Firstner of Stab IV/NJG1, he claimed a Lancaster or a Halifax west-north-west of Mönchengladbach at an altitude of 2,800 metres, although both this claim and that of Fritz Lau (see above) could be interchangeable. A third pilot may also have been responsible. Hauptmann Heinz-Horst Hissbach of 5/NJG2 claiming a Lancaster in the same area and about the same altitude at 22:05hrs (BST).

No. 619 Squadron lost Lancaster PB405 (PG-S) at 22:05hrs (BST) when it was shot down by a night-fighter and crashed between Roggel and Heythuysen, south-east of Eindhoven. Again, Hissbach, Lau, or even Greiner's victory claims may have been responsible for the loss of this aircraft and its crew of eight who were killed.

The four Lancasters lost, were almost certainly due to night-fighter activity, although a flak unit did make a claim which indicates there was some flak in operation around the area of the targets. The aerial combats reportedly took place at altitudes between 2,600 and 3,500 metres (8,530 to 11,483 feet) – well above the suspected altitude of Guy Gibson and the Mosquitos of No. 627 Squadron. According to surviving Luftwaffe combat records, no claims were made for a Mosquito by any German night-fighter crew that night and that includes claims to have damaged one.

Most researchers and historians have always claimed most of the Luftwaffe night-fighter records survived from this period, but can we be certain of this?

The Luftwaffe had scrambled a force of thirty-two Junkers 88s and Messerschmitt 110s from III/NJG1, IV/NJG1, Stab/NJG2 and II/NJG2 at Dortmund and Cologne-Butzweilerhof airfields between 21:17 and 21:57hrs (BST). In addition, Hauptmann Schmidt of 8/NJG1 was scrambled in his Messerschmitt 110 at 21:30hrs (BST) and eleven Junkers 88's of 1/NJG4 from Zellhausen were sent up at 21:10 until 22:35hrs (BST), when they were recalled after failing to make contact with the main bomber stream.

This was a sizable night-fighter force, but it was clearly handicapped by an early warning system which had been degraded by mid-September 1944. The RAF also utilised the *Window* radar jamming tactics and radio operators giving false instructions to the night-fighters.

The German night-fighters operated among the bomber stream and few if any, would fly at the lower Mosquito target marker altitudes. This was partly due to the abilities of the fighter pilots and also the possibility of light flak. It is important to note, that no German night-fighters were reportedly lost that night, although we have no reports of combat damage sustained by them.

Although only four Lancasters were shot down, Bomber Command intelligence reported a good number of combat claims and sightings of enemy or unidentified aircraft. Between 21:48 and 21:53hrs (BST), four No. 106 Squadron crews reported enemy aircraft and seeing a number of falling Lancasters. A Focke Wulf 190, Messerschmitt 110 and a Junkers 88 were all reported over Rheydt at 10,300 feet. One crew reported seeing a Lancaster on their starboard bow, falling in flames from an altitude of 10,400 feet over the town at 21:52hrs. Other crews seem to have sighted the same falling Lancaster around this time. This machine was possibly one of their own squadron (PB359 coded ZN-T), although one crew at 22:03hrs may have seen the destruction of the single No. 619 Squadron machine.

Various crews from Nos. 57, 44, 207 and 630 Squadrons reported seeing a number of enemy aircraft at altitudes between 11,800 and 13,700 feet over Mönchengladbach and Rheydt. One crew from No. 630 Squadron reported seeing a Lancaster with a Messerschmitt 110 on its tail, before observing an explosion on the ground two minutes later.

A crew from No. 106 Squadron (aircraft ZT-H) and a crew from No. 83 Squadron (aircraft H), reported seeing an aircraft falling in flames. The No. 106 Squadron crew's sighting occurred at 22:11hrs (BST) at an altitude of 9,000 feet north-west of Brecht (east of Antwerp in Belgium). They were on their way home when they saw an aircraft on their port side going down in flames before it exploded on the ground. Prior to this, at 21:59hrs (BST), the 83 Squadron crew reported seeing at 13,000 feet, between Geel and Mol in Belgium, an aircraft going down in flames and hitting the ground after an apparent air-to-air combat. It appears both aircraft might have been slightly mistaken in their position and they had in fact witnessed the loss of the No. 467 Squadron Lancaster which crashed at this time, just over the border and south-west of Eindhoven.

Apart from the aircraft near Eindhoven, no other allied aircraft crashed in Holland that night apart from the Mosquito of Gibson and Warwick.

In terms of possible sighting of Gibson's aircraft there are a number of possible reports that may have been his Mosquito.

At 22:20hrs (BST) the crew of a No. 106 Squadron Lancaster (ZT-H), who had already seen an aircraft falling in flames (see above), reported seeing another aircraft to their starboard side falling in flames. They gave their altitude as 9,000 feet and their position at that time as 51.48N / 04.05E. This position is near Yerseke on the island of Zeeland, about fifteen miles south-west of Gibson's crash site at Steenbergen. If they were on an expected north-westerly track back towards Lincolnshire, the falling aircraft sighted could have been close to Steenbergen.

At the same time, the crew of No. 97 Squadron's commanding officer, Wing Commander Baker, reported seeing an aircraft shot down, which burst into flames on the ground with a red flame that turned yellow. The crew were at an altitude of 11,000 feet and a reported position of 51.35N / 04.20E. This is over Antwerp docks and about fifteen to twenty miles south of

Steenbergen. What they meant by 'shot down' is unclear and we do not know whether they saw gun fire and tracer, but it seems very likely.

Is it possible the two Lancaster crews could have seen the disabled Mosquito flown by Gibson and Warwick crash at Steenbergen? The location appears to be correct, but neither crew gives an indication of the height of the doomed aircraft or its direction of flight.

The reported timings for this incident are a possible issue. If correct, the two Lancaster crews saw a doomed aircraft, approximately ten minutes before the reported time Gibson's Mosquito crashed at Steenbergen. While the Mosquito may have been damaged and circling for a time, the timings appear to be too early, as the two Lancaster crews reported seeing the resultant crash. There is also no mention of the time lapse between the aircraft being shot down and when it made contact with the ground. However, we must be careful with timings, as one person's clock could be slow and another person's fast, leading to a time that is incorrect by anything up to five or more minutes. There is also no evidence of another aircraft crashing in that area that night, so it appears to have been the Mosquito of Gibson and Warwick.

It is very easy to assume the red and yellow flames seen by the No. 97 Squadron crew may have been Gibson's hung-up and unused target indicators burning on the ground, but we cannot say for certain.

Flight Sergeant John Foster Thorp, a rear gunner with No. 467 Squadron and part of Flight Lieutenant McLauchlan's crew, bombed Rheydt at 21:50hrs (BST). They bombed the green TIs from 10,300 feet and headed for home. In an audio statement held by the International Bomber Command Centre, Thorp states that as they were coming home across Holland, he looked down and saw a twin-engine aircraft on fire. It was flying while on fire. It was obviously under control because he thought it was trying to make a forced land. He saw it hit the ground and burst into flames. He was told after they had returned, that Guy Gibson was missing and after some time, he started to connect the two incidents.

Unfortunately, John Thorp did not give a specific location or time for his sighting, but if no German fighters or other allied twin engine aircraft were lost that night, we can assume this may have been Guy Gibson's Mosquito.

In her book '*Dambuster*' on page 163, author Susan Ottaway cites a possibility Gibson had lost an engine and this may have been the cause of his crash.

Susan Ottaway states, 'Perhaps the most puzzling story is that told by the crew of a 61 Squadron Lancaster.' The crew had heard Gibson give them and other crews a verbal pat on the back and send them on their way home. Minutes later they again heard Gibson's voice state that he had lost an engine and was losing height. His final words were allegedly, 'I'm trying to make it home.' Nothing more was heard from him. He did not seem distressed and the de Havilland Mosquito was more than capable of returning home on one engine.

It is unknown whether this loss of an engine was due to flak, a night-fighter or a technical issue, but whatever the cause, if correct, this could account for his demise.

What is interesting is that Susan Ottaway does not give specific details of the reference for this comment or allegation from this crew. She does provide a photographic image of the Lancaster crew and names only one of the crew members, the mid-upper gunner Sergeant John Aldridge, who completed his tour of operations that night. Although he cannot be confirmed as the source of this account, it appears likely.

What is perplexing is the fact the No. 61 Squadron Operations Record Book and its summary, contains no mention of this report (see ref: AIR 27/579/18 and AIR 27/579/17). Neither is there anything in the attached appendix of various forms and combat reports in the UK National Archives (reference AIR 27/582/01). This only contains two combat reports, one of which belongs to Sergeant Bernard McCormack and his crew, which we shall look at in a moment.

According to the records, Sergeant John Aldridge and his crew left RAF Skellingthorpe at 18:42hrs (BST) and returned home at 23:15hrs (BST). Their Lancaster, serial number PD199, was crewed by Flying Officer H.L. Inniss (pilot), Sergeant H.T. Ansell (flight engineer), Flying Officers J.T.O. Dickinson (navigator), J.R. Morrison (bomb aimer), Sergeant K.F. Moseley (wireless operator) and Flight Sergeant R.R. Langley (rear gunner).

According to the squadron's Operations Record Book, Aldridge and his crew bombed the green target indicators at 21:50hrs (BST) from an altitude of 10,000 feet. The Red Force Controller (Guy Gibson) gave orders to bomb the green force aiming point at 21:48hrs. Concentrated bombing was seen on the yellow force aiming point, but little was seen of any other bombing. The aiming point was not clearly identified, but fires appeared to be burning in town's built-up areas.

As we have seen in a previous chapter, Flying Officer John Humphreys, a flight engineer with No. 97 Squadron, reported that Gibson flew across the Rheydt aiming point flashing his navigation lights. It is surprising no one else mentions this, but if Gibson did this, he was likely to attract the attention of the flak gunners and any German night-fighter pilot willing to drop down to a lower altitude over the town.

In October 2011, the BBC and the *Daily Mail,* among other media outlets, reported that Guy Gibson's death had been caused by friendly fire. They claimed a movie producer – James Cutler – who was undertaking research for a proposed remake of the Dambusters film, had uncovered an audio tape made by a mid-upper gunner in No. 61 Squadron. The gunner claimed to have mistakenly shot Guy Gibson down that night.

James Cutler wrote an article on his discovery for *Britain at War* magazine in October 2011. He spoke with Eunice McCormack, the widow of Sergeant Bernard McCormack, who claimed that in the 1980s she attended an aircrew reunion and heard her husband talking with ex-comrades about how 'they had shot down Guy Gibson'. Eunice, in time, aware of the importance of her husband's claim, secretly recorded him discussing the incident in their home.

James Cutler obtained a copy of the tape recording from the air gunner's wife and she also showed him her late husband's flying logbook, which clearly displayed a claim for a probable Junkers 88 that night. Bernard McCormack had died in 1992, but on the tape cassette, he can be heard recalling how he fired off 600 rounds at what he thought was a Junkers 88 night-fighter. McCormack stated:

> 'All of a sudden, this kite comes right behind us, twin engines and a single rudder, and it comes bouncing in towards us so we opened fire and we blew him up.... When we got back, we claimed a JU88 shot down. The following day we were quizzed again and the officer asked, "What made you think it was a JU88?" We said, it had twin engines and a single rudder, but the officer said, "So has a Mosquito, supposing his radio and his radar was knocked out and he was lost and he spotted a Lancaster – he would only want to follow it home, wouldn't he?"'

The main issue with this audio recording is the mention of the aircraft blowing up – what exactly did Bernard McCormack mean by this? Most people would think it means the enemy aircraft blew up and disintegrated into many pieces. If that was the case, it could not have been Guy Gibson's Mosquito, so did he mean an engine burst into flame? We will never know, but as we shall see these claims are not consistent with the combat report for this crew held in the UK National Archives.

Although the main Operations Record Book for No. 61 Squadron says there were no enemy fighters encountered by the unit that night, in the index file there is a combat report from Bernard McCormack's crew detailing their claim for a Junkers 88.

The report held in UK National Archives file (reference AIR 27/582), states that at 22:25hrs (BST) at 10,000 feet at position 51.51N / 04.00E they spotted a Junkers 88 night-fighter. This position is near Yerseke on Zeeland and the report from the 106 Squadron crew (ZT-H) of an aircraft to their starboard side seen falling in flames. It is also not far from the aircraft reportedly seen shot down by the 97 Squadron crew at a similar time which crashed and burned with a red and then yellow flame. John Thorp, the 467 Squadron gunner, also saw a burning twin engine aircraft on fire below them over Holland. Although he does not give a precise position or time for his sighting, his aircraft bombed the target at a similar time to the 97 and 106 squadron crews and therefore he could have been in the same area over Holland, when he saw the burning aircraft.

According to the No. 61 Squadron combat report, the enemy aircraft was first seen ahead of the Lancaster at a lower altitude by the bomb aimer in the nose of the Lancaster. The enemy aircraft also allegedly had its navigation lights on according to the report.

The mid-upper gunner (Sergeant Bernard McCormack) saw the enemy aircraft to their starboard side and opened fire, before the rear gunner Sergeant Maudersley also opened up. The enemy fighter moved into a position behind the Lancaster – dead astern at a range of about 400 yards. As the fighter approached to 300 yards it opened fire, before breaking off at a range of about 200 yards.

The pilot of the Lancaster had entered the standard corkscrew evasive manoeuvre and both McCormack and Maudersley opened fire again. Both gunners reported observing strikes on the enemy aircraft which broke away and dived to port. No mention was made in the combat report of the aircraft blowing up or fire being observed and the two gunners claimed the Junkers 88 as only damaged and not destroyed.

While James Cutler and the media claim this could account for Guy Gibson's loss that night, there are a number of issues with this story:

- Firstly, Guy Gibson's Mosquito had no guns and he could not have opened fire, although the gunners may have believed the 'Junkers 88' had opened fire.
- Secondly, the crew claimed the JU88 as damaged, not destroyed or probably destroyed. They also claimed in their report that the JU88 had its navigation lights on. This complicates matters as we have already heard that Gibson had flashed his lights over the target and a number of Lancasters had their lights on during and after the raid.
- Thirdly, Bernard McCormack's flying logbook states he made a claim for a probable JU88, not one destroyed or damaged.
- Fourthly, the aircraft approached the Lancaster from head on. If they were heading home to England and about to cross the Dutch coastline, the fighter was heading in the opposite direction and back towards Germany – why would Gibson's Mosquito be heading in that direction?
- Fifthly, the altitude of the combat seems to be at odds with the accepted version of events, as Gibson was going

to fly home across Holland at low-level and not at 10,000 feet.

- Finally, McCormack and his crew did not see the aircraft crash or report it being on fire as it dived away.

According to the secret Bomber Command intelligence report for the night of the 19-20 September 1944 (see reference UK National Archives AIR 24/294), the enemy defences accounted for five aircraft. It states: 'Flak was moderate and no enemy aircraft were claimed as destroyed.' The comment about no enemy aircraft being claimed as destroyed, clearly does not count Bernard McCormack and his crew's claims to have damaged a Junkers 88.

When the report was written on 2 February 1945, nearly five months after the raid, the intelligence officers noted that four aircraft fell to enemy fighters – two over the target, a third near Turnhout in Belgium and a fourth over the Dutch Islands. The fifth was lost without trace. Two aircraft were damaged by flak and two by enemy fighters. These comments were written after Steenbergen had been liberated and Guy Gibson's aircraft had been located and his death confirmed.

The intelligence report appears to confirm the two No. 106 Squadron aircraft brought down near Mönchengladbach and Rheydt, and either No. 467 or No. 619 Squadron's aircraft near Eindhoven. It therefore appears they are possibly including Gibson's Mosquito as the fourth aircraft brought down by enemy fighters, but on what evidence?

The Night Bombing raid sheet No. 2438 (see AIR 14/2679 in the UK National Archives) completed shortly after the raid, states that two Lancasters from No. 5 Group were damaged by enemy fighters and another two by flak. Six Lancasters reported being attacked by a night-fighter, while another five sighted a fighter, but were not attacked.

Bernard McCormack and his crew would have been debriefed after landing. We cannot say exactly when their combat report was completed, but there is another one in the file from a second No. 61 Squadron crew that night. They reported engaging a Junkers 88 south of Eindhoven at an altitude of 8,500 feet at about 22:02hrs (BST). The two gunners on this Lancaster opened fire, but made no claim was made for the Junkers 88.

Bernard McCormack claimed he was reinterviewed with his crew the next day by an intelligence officer who questioned whether the Junkers 88 could have been a Mosquito.

It appears on face value, very unlikely the authorities seriously considered the claim of a damaged Junkers 88 by McCormack and his crew, as sufficient evidence to believe they were responsible for shooting down Guy Gibson. The authorities at that time did not know Gibson was dead and had come down at Steenbergen, neither did they have access to Luftwaffe loss records.

The belief among some historians and researchers, that this information was in some way covered up and hidden in the No. 61 Squadron ORB appendix, is also hard to believe. Even if they had considered this as the possible cause for the loss, it stretches the imagination to believe they then hid this information, as it would be weeks before the site of the crash was liberated and the various pieces of information could be put together.

However, there is another strange twist to the account of Bernard McCormack and his crew.

Warrant Officer Donald Ross Souter, the pilot of McCormack's Lancaster, was later commissioned and awarded a Distinguished Flying Cross in March 1945. The original recommendation in December 1944 and the later citation, mentioned a number of incidents of note, but also the following:

> 'Flying Officer Souter has completed twenty-eight successful sorties comprising 168 hours of operational flying, including many attacks on German targets such as Stettin, Darmstadt (twice), Koenigsburg (twice), Wilhelmshaven, Bremen, Dusseldorf and Hamburg.
>
> 'On the night of the 19/20 September 1944, after a successful attack on Rheydt, on the homeward journey Flying Officer Souter's aircraft was attacked by an enemy night-fighter which resulted in extensive damage to both fins and rudders of his aircraft. By skilful handling of his aircraft and despite the damage sustained, the enemy aircraft was engaged, damaged and driven off. Flying Officer Souter then flew his aircraft back to base and landed it safely.'

Clearly, this throws a completely different complexion on the combat report submitted by Bernard McCormack and the crew on the night of 19–20 September 1944. There is no mention in their combat report or the unit's Operations Record Books of any damage to their Lancaster, so why was this listed in Donald Souter's DFC citation? The award and the citation were also reported in the *Calgary Herald* newspaper, Souter's home city in Canada.

It has been suggested that Bomber Command were trying to cover-up the loss of Guy Gibson and it being due to so-called friendly fire. However, I have examined in detail the Operations Record Book for No. 61 Squadron and its appendix which contains a good number of combat reports from various crews. I cannot find another combat report in September 1944, that relates to Warrant Officer Souter and Sergeant Bernard McCormack. Neither can I find any reference to damage being sustained by their Lancaster that month and although ground crews worked miracles to repair damaged aircraft, there is no evidence their Lancaster was damaged and taken off operations for repairs.

I shall further examine the issue of a cover-up in the next chapter.

While the Luftwaffe fighters made no claims for a Mosquito that night, there were a number of sorties flown by British night-fighters, their aim being to protect the main bomber force.

Night Operations sheet No. 2447 held in the UK National Archives (reference AIR 24/2679), states that seventeen Mosquitos from No. 100 Group were deployed that night. Sixteen flew intruder patrols near enemy airfields, while just one Mosquito was sent on a Serrate sortie, but no incidents were noted and there were no claims made for the destruction or even the damaging of an enemy aircraft. (Serrate was a radar system used to home in on German night-fighter radar emissions.)

The No. 100 Group Night-fighter weekly summary No. 61 for the week ending 22/23 September 1944, gives very little detail about the evening of 19 September. (See reference AIR 14/3323 in the UK National Archives.)

While some may believe Gibson and Warwick were brought down by Sergeant McCormack and his crew, the evidence, in my opinion, is not that convincing for the reasons I have set out. Neither is there any evidence he was brought down by an RAF night-fighter.

The next possible cause for the crash is a technical fault or problem. This is a difficult area to consider as we have no evidence there was a problem with the aircraft. Although we have heard one witness report that they heard Gibson say he had lost an engine, no one else reported this and no one reported seeing anything wrong with Gibson's Mosquito over the target.

It is possible something went wrong with the aircraft after it left the target, but we will never know as the wreckage was not examined in 1944 and as we shall see later, it was too late for a methodical examination when the site was excavated at the end of 1985.

As already discussed, the loss of one engine should not have been too much of an issue for Gibson, as a Mosquito could fly on one engine. The question is whether he could handle a one-engine Mosquito with his limited experience on the type?

The issue of a technical problem brings us nicely onto the next possible cause – that of pilot or crew error.

We know Gibson had very limited flying time on the Mosquito despite his lengthy career and undoubted flying skills. Gibson is believed to have amassed approximately thirteen hours on Mosquitos, while his navigator had no experience at all on this type of aircraft. A No. 627 Squadron engineering officer had apparently tried to brief James Warwick about his role in the Mosquitos cockpit, before an impatient Gibson 'threw him out.' James Warwick was not only responsible in the aircraft for navigation, but also the radio and more importantly, the fuel management processes.

The aircraft Gibson and Warwick operated that night was a Mosquito B.XX serial number KB267. This aircraft and the discarded Mosquito KB213, were built in Canada and used American Packard Merlin engines rather than the standard Rolls-Royce Merlin engines of other British built Mosquitos.

Unlike the British Merlin engines, the American Packard Merlin engines on Mosquito KB267, had pressure carburettors similar to a fuel injection system. To start the engines meant switching on the fuel pressure pump. Gibson had flown a B.XX model before, as well as the British model, but the real issue was the fuel transfer switches and their process which was completely alien to James Warwick.

The gun-less Mosquito B.XX, had fuel transfer switches located on the bulkhead at the rear of the cockpit, behind the navigator's seat and the radio set. The navigator would have to lean back to move these switches and control the flow of fuel between the various tanks. The Mosquito had outer wing fuel tanks, outside of each engine nacelle and two more main wing tanks, positioned one in each wing between the fuselage and the engine nacelles. In the fuselage there were two more main fuel tanks.

The Mosquito would take off using the main tanks in its fuselage. Once airborne the crew would switch over to use the fuel from the two outer tanks in the wings. Once these outer wing tanks were drained, the remaining fuel in the main wing tanks in-board of the engines would be used, followed by that in the fuselage. The navigator, in this case James Warwick, was responsible at the behest of Guy Gibson in switching these tank switches back and forth during the flight and ensuring the correct flow of fuel to the engines.

Over the many years since the crash, experts have speculated about the fuel system causing problems for James Warwick and there being a shortage of fuel to the engines, either though accidental mismanagement by the inexperienced navigator or he was incapacitated in some way, possibly through injury or even death. In addition, damage to one or more of the fuel tanks may have caused a loss of fuel which complicated the management situation for Warwick. Fuel starvation for the engines has therefore become one of the most speculated causes for this crash.

Other researchers have worked out that the Mosquito flying at its cruise speed, would have required a switch from the outer tanks to the main wing tanks before it reached the target in Germany. If Warwick and Gibson had failed to deal with that simple operation, they would not have been able to undertake the Controller's role over the target and headed back across Holland.

If they only used the main tanks they would not have run out of fuel. The fuel permutations and calculations are varied and laborious, but the simple fact is one way or another, it is unlikely the failure to manage the fuel correctly resulted in the loss of the aircraft; unless of course Warwick or Gibson were incapacitated in some way or dead.

The fact witnesses saw the inside of the Mosquitos cockpit illuminated as it flew over Steenbergen is a curious one. The cockpit naturally had low-intensity lights to allow the operation of the aircraft and the instruments to be read, but the comments appear to indicate an overly bright illumination from something inside the cockpit. Was there a fire in the cockpit and what could have caused this? The Mosquito apparently still had its full complement of target indicators in its bomb bay, could one of these have ignited in some way and was burning its way into the cockpit?

Perhaps the most curious of all the possible explanations, is that of aircraft sabotage. In his 1991 book – *Ghost Stations IV*, author Bruce Barrymore Halpenny claimed to have received letters from a number of unnamed individuals reporting that Gibson's Mosquito 'had been interfered with.'

Bruce Barrymore Halpenny stated that Guy Gibson was not popular with ground crews and that the fuel pipe union nuts, leading to the carburation system, had been loosened. After a sustained period of flight and engine vibration, they eventually disconnected and covered the hot engine with fuel, causing a catastrophic fire for the mainly wooden aircraft.

Halpenny then named a former ground crewman who was at Coningsby that night and watched Gibson take off. This man claimed another airman had stated, 'I don't think we shall see Mr Gibson again somehow – it's been fixed well and truly this time.' The airmen said rumours then began to circulate that the fuel system had been interfered with. A few years later, Halpenny claimed to hear a very similar account from two more men when he overheard their conversation in a hotel lounge.

The problem with these claims is two-fold, one, Gibson took off from Woodhall Spa and not Coningsby and secondly and more importantly, he changed aircraft an hour before take-off. If someone had interfered with his original designated Mosquito (KB213), surely the crew of that machine would have crashed or at least reported an issue? As we have seen, KB213 was flown by the displaced crew of Flight Lieutenants Peter Mallender and Wallace Gaunt and they returned safely to Woodhall Spa.

There was also very little chance for someone to interfere with KB267 once it was allocated to Gibson and Warwick. It had already been prepared for flight and in the hour before take-off, once Gibson had decided to take it, the armourers were busy changing its load of target markers. There was therefore little opportunity for someone to tamper with the engines while the armourers changed the TIs. For these reasons, I believe the hypothesis of sabotage can be completely disregarded.

The final possible cause was the weather. A number of crews reported electrical storm conditions on the flight home and one crew reported heavy static. Those that reported this reported difficult flying conditions, but although a lighting-strike might bring an aircraft down with a blow to an engine in 1944, the chances are very slim and this is an unlikely cause.

Chapter Twelve

The Post War Scene Examination and Recovery

After the war, very little remained at the crash site to indicate the exact position where Gibson's Mosquito had crashed. For a number of years, the soil was a slightly different colour, but this was barely noticeable.

The Commonwealth War Graves Commission marked the graves of Guy Gibson and James Warwick with their standard Portland headstone markers, Gibson's being engraved with the Victoria Cross. Today, flowers and poppies are regularly placed on the graves and someone has added a small figurine of a labrador dog. The graves are well tended and cared for, the local population still holding the deceased in high regard.

The crash site was used over many decades for farming, but in the early 1980s a decision was made to extend the small post-war industrial site, which would eventually cover the location of the crash.

The people of Steenbergen to this day, fully recognise the significance of the crash site and on 11 October 1985, the Burgomaster and Eldermen of Steenbergen wrote to the Dutch military authorities asking them to conduct a recovery of whatever remains there were at the crash site. Their letter noted; 'Due to the special place which Guy Gibson does have in RAF history, and to prevent any difficulties which might arise when the area will be built over, we think the recovery is necessary.'

On 23 October, members of the Royal Netherlands Air Force attended the site and carried out a preliminary survey and assessment. They concluded in a report to their senior command that it was likely there was wreckage and other materials buried in the field that could be recovered. The examination of the crash site deduced that it was possible one or possibly parts of both engines, could be present in the earth and recoverable.

On 30 October 1985, the Recovery and Identification Officer of the Royal Netherlands Air Force wrote to the RAF giving the above facts. Although the report did not speculate on the possibility of human remains being found, it is clear they were aware of how few remains had been recovered and buried in September 1944. The Recovery and Identification Officer asked that Guy Gibson's widow, Eve Gibson, and the next of kin of Squadron Leader James Warwick be informed of the planned recovery operation. The officer also asked for confirmation of what explosives, in terms of flares and or bombs, the aircraft was carrying in September 1944, to assist the recovery team.

On 14 November 1985, the RAF informed the Dutch Recovery and Identification Officer that they had informed Eve Gibson. She was already aware this might happen and accepted the need for the recovery operation. Eve had also informed the sister of James Warwick with whom she was still in contact.

The RAF report added that Gibson's aircraft had carried seven target indicators plus flares that night. The available evidence indicates that Gibson did not drop any of these TIs, although reports from other crews indicated that he had a hung-up target indicator that night. The likelihood is the target indicators would have been consumed by the fire at the crash site, but the RAF report advised caution as there was a slight risk to any excavators.

The number of seven TIs is interesting, as the No. 627 Squadron aircraft, according to their Operations Record Book, were carrying up to four target indicators each, but if correct, Gibson was clearly carrying a smaller version of each target indicator.

On 11-12 December 1985, a Royal Netherlands Air Force recovery team arrived at the crash site in Steenbergen and started to excavate the location. An official from the British Embassy in The Hague attended (probably the Air Attaché) on both days and reported that no trace of the crew or their clothing was found during the excavation.

The recovery team consisted of an explosives removal team and a rapid runway repair equipment team, as well as the investigators and their diggers.

The excavation covered an area 40 feet square and to a depth of 9-12 feet. It was clear the Mosquito has crashed at a relatively high-speed and disintegrated upon impact with the ground, followed by an intense fire which had consumed most of the airframe. A few parts of the cockpit instruments were found, as well as one landing wheel and a shattered engine at a depth of about 3 metres (9-10 feet).

The subsequent Dutch salvage report recorded that several small pieces of wood and fabric, although severely rotten, were found in the earth. Small parts from the bomb bay, including bomb hooks, wiring and connections were also found. One undercarriage leg, complete but severely damaged, was also recovered along with some of the fuel tanks, part of the flaps, radiators and fuel hosing and pipes. Parts of one engine were recovered, but this had disintegrated upon impact with the ground, while plating from the starboard engine nacelle was also recovered.

One small section of the wooden fuselage was recovered on which the letters 'KB' from the aircraft's serial number (KB267) were still visible. The excavated remains were taken by military vehicles to Gilze-Rijen Air Force base a few miles away, where they were laid out in a hangar for cataloguing and evaluation.

The recovery team concluded that their findings confirmed eyewitness evidence from 1944, stating that most parts of the aircraft had been lying on top of the ground, scattered around and there had been a fire at the main impact point. From the available excavated wreckage, it was impossible to ascertain the reason for the crash, but the position in which parts were recovered, indicated the Mosquito must have impacted the ground in a steep dive, with the right wing low at a relatively high speed.

What is interesting, is there is no mention of any indication of battle damage to any of the recovered parts, including the fuel tanks. However, these remains were only a small part of the original aircraft structure and this does not mean enemy action can be ruled out as a cause in bringing down Guy Gibson's Mosquito that night.

Although the Dutch Air Force recovery report does not mention it specifically, James Cutler, in his *Britain at War* magazine article in 2011, states that a 'Burnt out target indicator flare' was found at the recovery site. How he knows this when the Dutch Air Force report held by the RAF Air Historical Branch does not contain this specific piece of information is unclear.

After a careful forensic examination of the wreckage, a number of items were sent to various museums. One large piece went to the RAF Staff College at Bracknell (an image of which is contained in the plate section of this book), while smaller parts of the fuselage went to RAF Metheringham. The piece of the fuselage bearing the part serial number 'KB' and part of the undercarriage, was displayed in the small museum at Metheringham.

At Steenbergen the expansion of the industrial site was given the go-ahead and soon completed. The exact location of the crash was marked with different coloured block paving to form a Union flag and the year 1944. A wooden post with a simple inscribed plaque gives the names and the date of the crash, as well as noting the fact Gibson led the Dambusters raid. It is an austere memorial, but it is difficult to adequately remember Guy Gibson and James Warwick in such a location and the local community have done their best and should be respected for this. This memorial is in Mosquito Straat, surrounded by warehouses and parking lots, adjacent roads being named Gibsonstraat and Warwickstraaat.

To the south of the town, there is a more fitting memorial in a park with a Lancasters propellor on top of a stone plinth with another inscribed plaque.

There is no evidence from the crash site that can support any of the theories concerning the loss of Guy Gibson's Mosquito that night. A forensic examination of any crash site over forty years after the incident would be difficult, but with the loss of a mainly wooden de Havilland Mosquito and an intense fire, it was almost impossible to find any worthwhile evidence. The 1985 excavation was more concerned with possible human remains being present than the cause of the crash. What we have left is a number of possible causes and Gibson's own behaviour in the lead up to the operation and during the raid itself.

Post crash, we are left with the question – 'Was there a cover-up?' It is very easy to suspect this with the combat report of Bernard McCormack and the fact it was allegedly hidden away in the Operations Record Book Appendix; but that is where all the other combat reports were held by No. 61 Squadron in the summer of 1944.

Perhaps the more confusing and mystifying fact is why and how Warrant Officer Ronald Souter's DFC citation mentions this particular operation and the serious damage to the Lancaster – despite it not appearing in the combat report or the Operations Record Book. Initially, I thought this might have been an administrative error and perhaps they sustained damage from a fighter on another sortie in September 1944, but I cannot find any trace of this on another date in the records.

These factors, together with the delayed official announcement of Guy Gibson's death, has often been used to suggest there was a possible friendly fire cover-up. Even Air Marshal Arthur 'Bomber' Harris was slow to send a telegram to No. 617 Squadron's Officers' Mess at Woodhall Spa. Despite this, we must remember that Guy Gibson would have been a major propaganda coup for the Nazis if he had survived and was in German hands. Even if he was identified as being killed, the Nazi regime would have boasted about this. The British had to be certain he was dead and not a prisoner of war.

Chapter Thirteen

The Direct and Indirect Cause of Death

In analysing any cause of death, there are often various direct and indirect issues and contributory factors. In air crash investigation, experts often state that the cause of a crash is more often than not the result of a series of factors or faults which combine to cause the crash.

In terms of Guy Gibson's death, there are any number of possible direct and non-direct causes and contributory factors which may have led to his demise.

We have looked at the direct causes and narrowed them down to one of a few possibilities. These included enemy flak, a so-called blue-on-blue friendly fire incident, a technical fault/issue, or the crew being unable to manage the aircraft, either through a lack of training and experience or incapacity.

There is no doubt that there were numerous concentrations of flak, especially low-level anti-aircraft fire, both over the target area and along Gibson's return route across Holland. This included the area of fighting during Operation Market Garden and around the Luftwaffe airfield at Gilze-Rijen (coincidentally the location the remains were sent to for analysis in 1985). Two Lancasters reportedly returned with flak damage, so we can assume the anti-aircraft defences were active, despite the degradation of recent weeks.

Although the de Havilland Mosquito could sustain serious damage, including the loss of an engine and remain airborne, any damage to a vital component part or the crew could bring it down. The problem with this hypothesis, is no flak gun crew or detachment claimed a Mosquito that night, although the damaged aircraft may have been able to fly out of sight of the gunners before catching fire and eventually crashing to earth. The distance between Gilze-Rijen airfield and Steenbergen is about thirty-five to forty miles or about ten minutes flying time if the Mosquito had a speed of about 240mph. In addition, there was very little left of the Mosquito in 1944 and even less when the site was excavated in 1985, this making any forensic examination regarding a likely cause impossible.

The likelihood of the Mosquito being brought down by a German night-fighter is even smaller. No Luftwaffe aircrew claimed a Mosquito that night, not even a damaged machine. The scalp of a de Havilland Mosquito was a highly prized victory and any Luftwaffe pilot would be only too keen to report engaging a Mosquito and bringing it down. They would also have been proud to have damaged one, so it is nigh on impossible a German night-fighter brought Gibson and Warwick down that night.

The Mosquitos of No. 100 Group who flew Serrate and Intruder missions that night did not make one claim, so they are unlikely to have been responsible for a friendly fire incident.

Whether Gibson and Warwick were brought down by friendly fire from a Lancaster bomber is a totally different issue. As we have seen there have been a number of proponents, some of them experts in military aviation, who firmly believe Gibson and Warwick were brought down by Sergeant Bernard McCormack and his No. 61 Squadron crew. However, I believe there are a couple of evidential issues with this hypothesis, they are:

- Guy Gibson's Mosquito had no guns and he could not have opened fire. Why the crew would report the approaching aircraft had opened fire is unclear, especially as there was no reported damage to their Lancaster – although that appears to have changed with the citation for their pilot Souter's DFC. Some people have speculated the crew reported the fighter to have opened fire to cover their own mistake, but they only claimed it damaged and did not know it had crashed.
- McCormack's crew only claimed the Junkers 88 as damaged, not destroyed or probably destroyed. They also claimed in the report that the Junkers 88 had its navigation lights on. This complicates matters as we have already heard Gibson had flashed his navigation lights over the target and a number of Lancasters also had their lights on during and after the raid.
- McCormack's recorded evidence many years after the incident also clouds and confuses the account. He stated, 'We opened fire and we blew him up. When we got back, we claimed a JU88 shot down.' The original combat report makes no mention of the fighter blowing up or being claimed as shot down, so how can we give any credit to this hypothesis?

- The Junkers 88 reportedly approached the Lancaster from head on. If they were en route home to England and about to cross the Dutch coastline, the enemy fighter was heading in the opposite direction and back towards Germany. If it was Gibson, why was he flying in that direction and not homewards?
- Finally, the Lancaster crew did not see the aircraft crash or report it being on fire as it dived away. There is no mention in the No. 61 Squadron Operation Record Book about shooting down or damaging a Junkers 88, but Brian Cull the author of *Blue on Blue the definitive study of friendly fire losses in WW2*, notes that in his experience, combat reports suggesting an incident of friendly-fire were often 'lost' or mislaid by the squadron concerned. The combat report from Bernard McCormack and his crew was hidden away in an appendix, but it appears all the squadron's air to air combat reports were held in this supplement to their ORB and they were not mislaid or lost.

It is for the above reasons that I cannot attribute the loss of Gibson and Warwick to a friendly-fire incident. However, the question is who did McCormack and his crew fire at that night? It is unlikely to have been a British night-fighter, they knew better than to approach a Lancaster over enemy territory, while surviving Luftwaffe records indicate that none of their night-fighters were known to have returned with battle damage following combat in that area. Does this mean the claimed Junkers 88 was another twin-engine aircraft, or is it possible the

Lancaster gunners missed and the night-fighter flew off looking for easier prey? It is worth bearing in mind that experienced German night-fighter pilots preferred to deal with a Lancaster crew who had not noticed their approach, rather than one corkscrewing across the sky with its gunners blazing away at them like this one. It is for this reason that many RAF bomber crews never saw the night-fighter which shot them down.

In terms of crew capability or incapacity, we know that Guy Gibson had little experience on the Mosquito, while James Warwick had none at all. As we have seen, it is unlikely there was an issue in just switching the flow of fuel from one tank to another, however, if the aircraft had been damaged by flak and there was a fuel leak, this might have necessitated a further switch over of the tanks mid-flight. Again, this might have been completed satisfactorily, but some people believe there may have been an issue of incapacity among the crew. If the aircraft had been damaged by flak and James Warwick was injured or even killed and there was a fuel leak, the aircraft could have run out of fuel. The question is what caused the fire seen by the witnesses just before the aircraft crashed?

At least two or three witnesses on the ground reported the aircraft making a whistling sound before it came down. In addition, at least two witnesses reported seeing the crew illuminated by a bright light emanating from inside the cockpit. Although we can no longer question the witnesses, it appears they were insistent the light came from inside the cockpit and not from the Mosquitos burning exterior. It is also clear from their descriptions, that the light was much brighter than the aircraft's normal interior lighting.

This brings us on to another hypothesis in relation to the hung-up target markers. We know Gibson had red, yellow and green TIs, as well as flares in his bomb bay. We also have reports that a red target indicator had hung-up when he tried to mark the aiming point at Rheydt. Is it therefore possible, that flak or other gun fire had ignited the candles in the TIs or flares and set them alight? Could the hung-up target indicator have ignited after they had left the target area?

The bomb bay was under the cockpit and the aircraft was mostly made of wood. Could the target indicators or flares have been burning in the bomb bay, before burning their way through the cockpit floor and into the wings and ultimately the engines? The flames could have entered the cockpit, illuminating the crew just before Gibson lost control and the aircraft crashed? We also have the claims of one Lancaster crew reporting an aircraft on fire crashing and a 'bright red fire like a TI' being observed followed by a yellow flame.

We will never know what directly caused Guy Gibson to crash that night, but I believe the most likely scenario is that he was hit while flying at low level by 20mm flak. This caused considerable damage to the Mosquito, possibly igniting the target indicators, flares and or the fuel lines/tanks. The whistling sound may have been air passing over or through holes caused by the flak. Both Guy Gibson and James Warwick may have been incapacitated from the flak and unable to control the aircraft. At such a low altitude they could not bale out, (assuming they were fit enough to have done this) and Gibson was left fighting to control the Mosquito while looking for a place to make a forced-landing. Eventually, Gibson lost control and the aircraft dived into the farm land and exploded in a ball of flame.

The non-direct contributing factors and causes are easier to identify. Guy Gibson was a man who was undoubtedly a victim of his own upbringing, social standing and circumstances. A young man from an unstable home, he was shipped off to a boarding school at a young age and he lost his mother in a terrible accident. Gibson's boarding school had strong traditional and religious values which he maintained until the end.

The fact he was somewhat opinionated and looked down on certain people and sections of society was indicative of Gibson's schooling and the 1930s RAF officer class he had entered before the war started. It is no surprise that many other witnesses recall another alumni of Gibson's old school (St. Edward's in Oxford), Douglas Bader, as being similarly outspoken and riven by class ideals and religion.

Guy Gibson and the pre-war officer class were still maintaining the inter-war class system in mid-1944, this being despite a sea change in attitudes and ideals throughout the war years. To Gibson, officers were a different class and social level to non-commissioned officers and certainly well above those employed in ground trades.

Gibson was a competitor and led from the front, first was first and second was nowhere as far as he was concerned. Failure would not be tolerated. As we have seen, Gibson was glad to bend a rule or two himself, but ultimately as a commanding officer, he was a strict disciplinarian who knew that while some rules could be bent, those that related to operations and winning the war were sacrosanct.

Although there is evidence that Gibson could be sympathetic and show some empathy when required, there is no doubt he wanted to personally succeed and in a bomber squadron, that meant the squadron he commanded had to succeed. Witness comments clearly indicate that Guy Gibson certainly measured a man by his decorations and rank.

Guy Gibson was keen to partake in Winston Churchill's tour of North America in the summer of 1943, he received adulation and was a household name across the Empire and North America, he was also the most highly decorated allied airmen at the time. When he returned home to Britain, he was forbidden to undertake operational flying and became office bound. He was like a caged tiger and became depressed, even reportedly driven to tears. Air Marshal Arthur Harris stated the North America tour had damaged Gibson, but the war had moved on in the few months he was away. Many men had come and gone, while technology and aircraft had rapidly advanced. In many ways, Gibson was now just a propaganda tool and no longer an operational bomber pilot.

Gibson dabbled in politics, but his heart was really with operational flying and 'his crews.' His operational appetite was whetted by his flight with a No. 630 Squadron crew, but his move to Coningsby and No. 54 Base would cause him real heart ache.

The altercation in No. 627 Squadron's Officers' Mess bar in July 1944, has never really been appreciated for what it was and what happened later. He was desperate to fly operations again, but the aircrew in the Officers' Mess were not impressed by his rank or medal ribbons and they cared even less when he asked, 'Don't you know who I am?' Bundled out of the bar and ceremonially debagged, it must have been a degrading shock for him after all the adulation he had received during his tour of North America.

Guy Gibson was a veteran pilot and leader, already ostracised from his beloved No. 617 Squadron, now he was being ignored and deemed of no importance to an elite Mosquito unit. To them he was a retired show pony, only good for propaganda purposes. This must have stung and hurt Gibson, only adding to his desire to fly operationally, preferably to show these men just how good he was.

The fact at least two navigators managed to escape flying with Guy Gibson on 19 September speaks volumes. Either they disliked the man or they feared he was not capable and or competent enough to undertake the role of a Pathfinder Controller that night.

This leads onto one of the most indelible, indirect causes which almost certainly contributed to the death of Guy Gibson on 19 September 1944 - the senior commanders of Bomber Command.

Whether that causation lays with the sympathetic local station commander, Air Commodore Alfred Sharp, the No. 5 Group Air Officer Commanding, Air Vice-Marshal Ralph Cochrane, or the Commander-in-Chief of Bomber Command, Air Marshal Arthur Harris; it is an undeniable fact they could have managed Guy Gibson and his need to fly operationally in a more astute manner.

As we have already seen, 'Bomber' Harris in his foreword to *Enemy Coast Ahead* mentioned the issue, adding that, 'He always had direct access to me, and on further pressure from him and his AOC, I quite wrongly allowed him to return to operations.'

Air Marshal Harris clearly blamed himself, but he also states that the No. 5 Group Air Officer Commanding (Ralph Cochrane) was also pressurising him on behalf of Guy Gibson.

There is no known written record by Air Commodore Alfred Sharp on the issue of Gibson and despite his comments at the start of *Enemy Coast Ahead,* Air Marshal Harris rarely commented again on the subject of the loss of his star pilot. In his book *Bomber Offensive,* first published in 1947 and re-published many times since, Arthur Harris only touches on the issue of Gibson and the Dams raid. No mention is made of his death or its circumstances. He certainly does not discuss the communications between himself, Gibson and Cochrane.

Air Vice-Marshal Ralph Cochrane is also difficult to pin down with a written record concerning the loss of Guy Gibson. One record that does exist is an essay he wrote on Guy Gibson, published in the 1959 Oxford University Press publication: *Dictionary of National Biography 1941-1950.* In the text Ralph Cochrane states:

> 'For some weeks Gibson strove hard for permission to fly on operations, but with a firm refusal. However, on the night of the 19-20 September 1944, when the main Lancaster force of No. 5 Group was attacking a target involving only slight penetration into enemy held territory, it was agreed he should fly in a Mosquito and act as "master bomber." Gibson successfully directed the attack, wished the force "good night" and turned for home in the normal manner. He did not reach home ....'

Some historians have discussed the fact Air Commodore Alfred Sharp was allegedly absent from RAF Coningsby on the evening of 19 September, and that Gibson possibly took advantage of the situation to appoint himself controller on the raid. It seems clear, both Harris and Cochrane state in their own written words, that permission was given for Guy Gibson to undertake his final operation, although both put a slightly different slant on their own interpretation of events. The question is, when exactly was Guy Gibson authorised to go on this raid, what his authorised role entailed and when was he told this and by whom?

It appears Gibson was due to fly that night having test flown the Coningsby based Mosquito that morning. At the time, the planned raid on Bremerhaven was still 'on' so was he expecting to go to Bremerhaven?

Gibson had lunch in the Officers' Mess with a crew from No. 97 Squadron at Coningsby and clearly expected to be on the raid that night, but he needed a different Mosquito and one was obtained from Woodhall Spa.

Things started to unravel when his deputed No. 627 Squadron navigator went sick and he had to find a replacement. Other candidates allegedly made themselves disappear until the unfortunate James Warwick was found and designated Gibson's navigator.

Mid-afternoon the raid to Bremerhaven was cancelled and a new target of Rheydt and Mönchengladbach designated. This, together with the change of aircraft, a lack of a navigator and the complicated plan, will have put increased pressure on

Gibson. When Eve telephoned him, he was irritated and clearly under some pressure.

If, as suggested, there were murmurings at the various briefings about Gibson's inclusion as the raid Controller, this would also have further agitated Gibson if he heard them at his own pre-raid briefing.

When he arrived at Woodhall Spa with Warwick, Gibson, for some unknown reason, discarded Mosquito KB213, an aircraft he had flown before. This caused some disagreement and further irritation between himself and No. 627 Squadron personnel.

As we have seen, the raid was somewhat confused and stressful with engine problems (Red marker 1) and hung-up target indicators, all of which would have further irritated Gibson.

Gibson's lack of training may have been an indirect contributory factor in his death. Gibson had only flown approximately thirteen hours in a Mosquito before 19 September, while undertaking just a few dive-bombing practice flights with Wing Commander Johnny Woodroffe. He had not received any structured formal training on the Mosquito, despite being told by Cochrane to receive adequate training at the Pathfinder unit at Warboys; perhaps with a couple of low-level bombing attacks on the practice range.

The renowned Pathfinder Hamish Mahaddie claimed in his book *Hamish,* that Guy Gibson rejected Cochrane's directions for training and was lost on the raid to Rheydt and Mönchengladbach. Mahaddie added that if Air Vice-Marshal

Ralph Cochrane had known Gibson had not been adequately trained, he would have prevented Gibson from flying that night.

Despite this information, Hamish Mahaddie believed Gibson to be a great bomber pilot and at the time of the Dams raid, to have been an exceptional pilot and leader.

Guy Gibson, despite being a strict disciplinarian with the squadrons he commanded, had shown in earlier times a propensity to break the odd rule. It is therefore no surprise, that after being told he could not fly operationally without the necessary Pathfinder training by his Group Commander, Ralph Cochrane, he still went on this final operation. He also ignored orders to remain above 10,000 feet and the advice from the experienced marker and friend Squadron Leader Charles Owen, to come back via the longer route over allied occupied Belgium.

Finally, is it possible Gibson, in one last attempt to upstage Leonard Cheshire – the man who took command of *his* squadron, devised low-level target marking and became something of a favourite with Ralph Cochrane – took matters too far? Could the fact, Cheshire was now the most highly decorated airman in the RAF, proclaimed by the media as the greatest bomber pilot of all and the Pathfinder genius, have been too much for Gibson? Could this, together with his lack of formal training, an inexperienced Mosquito navigator and a low-level dash across a heavily defended area have led to Gibson's death?

Although we cannot say exactly why Guy Gibson crashed that night in September 1944, we can say that he was certainly desperate to prove his worth, his abilities and flying skills to everyone. He was undoubtedly a very brave and courageous man, but he was headstrong and possibly thought he was better than many of his fellow aviators. His apparently over-inflated ego was allowed to go virtually unchecked by his senior commanders, who appear to have turned a 'blind-eye' to him going on a number of unauthorised flights, ultimately leading to this final fatal operation.

We should remember Guy Gibson as a brave young man, performing a difficult and dangerous wartime role. He had his faults like all human beings, but he was a man who performed numerous courageous acts, commanding and leading one of the most famous bombing raids in history. He led by example, staring the enemy in the face.

Although the *Dambusters* movie and a plethora of early post war books painted Guy Gibson as a daring leader and hero, I think we should remember him as a brave young man who had just turned twenty-six years when he died. He, like many of us, had his own frailties and marriage issues. He loved and lost his dog on the day of his most notable operation, a raid in which he lost a number of very close friends.

Guy Gibson is a hero to the British people, someone who led the Dambusters and died in service. Unlike Horatio Nelson, he did not die at the moment of victory. Instead, he was a man who could have remained safely on the ground, he could have entered politics and who knows where that may have led after peace was declared in 1945. We only have to look at his successor at No. 617 Squadron, to see what he could have been after the war. Leonard Cheshire, among other things, created a number of homes for the sick and disabled, as well as becoming a philanthropist. He was later made Baron Cheshire.

While we cannot say what brought down Guy Gibson and his navigator James Warwick that night, it is arguable that his own actions and the inaction of certain senior commanders may have led indirectly to his death.

Resources Used In This Book

Bibliography:

Michael Allen: *Pursuit Through Darkened Skies*, Crowood Press Ltd., 1999.
Ralph Barker: *Strike Hard, Strike Sure*, Pan Books, 1965.
Donald Bennett CB, CBE, DSO: *Pathfinder*, Goodall Publications, 1958/1988.
Theo Boiten: *Nachtjagd combat archive 1944 part 4*, Red Kite Books, 2021.
Bowman & Cushing: *Confounding the Reich*, Patrick Stephens Limited, 1996.
John Braham: *Night Fighter*, Bantam Books, 1961.
Martyn Chorlton: *The RAF Pathfinders*, Countryside Books, 2012.
Alan Cooper: *Born Leader*, Independent Books, 1993.
Jan van den Dreiesschen: *We Will Remember Them*, Erskine Press, 1979.
John Foreman: *RAF Fighter Command Victory Claims of WW2*, Red Kite, 2012.
Norman Franks: *RAF Fighter Command Losses - WW2*, Midland Publishing, 2000.
Guy Gibson: *Enemy Coast Ahead*, various, 1946.
Bruce Barrymore Halpenny: *Ghost Stations IV*, Casdec Publishing, 1992.
Sir Arthur Harris: *Bomber Offensive*, Frontline Books, 1998 (original 1947).
Peter Hinchcliffe: *The Other Battle, Luftwaffe Aces vs Bomber Command*, Air-life Publishing, 1996.
Hamish Mahaddie: *Hamish: The Story of a Pathfinder*, Ian Allen Books, 1989.
Middlebrook & Everitt: *The Bomber Command Diaries*, 1995.
M.S. Morgan: *Bad Hat Squadron – 29 Sqn at West Malling 1941-43*, (Amazon).
Richard Morris: *Guy Gibson*, Penguin Books, 1994.
Susan Ottaway: *Dambuster, The Life of Guy Gibson*, Pen & Sword Books, 1994.
Simon Parry: *Intruders over Britain*, Air Research Books, 1987.
David Price: *Mosquito Men*, Head of Zeus Books, 2022.
John Searby: *The Everlasting Arms*, William Kimber Books, 1988.
Christopher Shores: *Those Other Eagles*, Grub Street Books, 2004.
John Sweetman: *The Dams Raid: Epic or Myth*, Janes Publishing, 1982.
Wickham, Williams & Legg: *Dictionary of National Biography 1941-1950*, published by Oxford University Press, 1959.

Magazines & Newspapers:

Britain At War, October 2011 edition, by James Cutler.
Daily Mirror, 30 April 2015.

Daily Mail, 11 October 2011.
Daily Mail, 23 October 2010.
Aeroplane Monthly magazine, May & June 1977, September & October 1992.
Dambusters Remembered, *Grantham Journal*, 1993.
Gloucestershire Echo, 8 September 1944.
Derby Daily Mail, 8 September 1944.
Daily Record, 9 September 1944.
Daily News (London), 9 September 1944.
Birmingham Post, 9 September 1944.

UK National Archives:

The following references have been used in this book under version 3.0 of the Open Government Licence. The UK National Archives may, from time to time, issue new versions of the Open Government Licence. If you are already using information under a previous version of the Open Government Licence, the terms of that licence will continue to apply.

These terms are compatible with the Creative Commons Attribution License 4.0 and the Open Data Commons Attribution License, both of which license copyright and database rights. This means that when the information is adapted and licensed under either of those licences, you automatically satisfy the conditions of the OGL when you comply with the other licence. The OGLv3.0 is Open Definition compliant.

AIR 14/868 No. 5 Group Target Marking Procedures.
AIR 14/1213 Bomber Command Target Codes.
AIR 14/2145 Intelligence Watch Diary No. 5 Group Volume VII.
AIR 14/2679 Night Bombing Sheets, September 1944.
AIR 14/3323 100 Group Reports on Serrate Operations.
AIR 14/3412 Night Raid Report for 19-20 September 1944.
AIR 22/203 War Room Manual of Bomber Command Ops.
AIR 24/294 Night Raid Reports.
AIR 24/295 Bomber Command Intelligence 19/9/1944.
AIR 24/296 Bomber Command Intelligence Reports.
AIR 25/110 No. 5 Group HQ ORB.
AIR 27/288 Operations Record Book 29 Squadron.
AIR 27/288 Operations Record Book 515 Squadron.
AIR 27/290 Operations Record Book 29 Squadron.
AIR 27/342 Operations Record Book 29 Squadron.
AIR 27/482 Operations Record Book 49 Squadron.
AIR 27/487 Operations Record Book 50 Squadron.
AIR 27/539 Operations Record Book 57 Squadron.
AIR 27/579 Operations Record Book 61 Squadron.
AIR 27/579/17 No. 61 Squadron Operations Record Book, Appendix of reports.
AIR 27/686 Operations Record Book 83 Squadron.

AIR 27/688 Operations Record Book 83 Squadron.
AIR 27/691 Operations Record Book Index 83 Squadron.
AIR 27/706 Operations Record Book 85 Squadron.
AIR 27/707 Operations Record Book 85 Squadron.
AIR 27/768 Operations Record Book 97 Squadron.
AIR 27/803 Operations Record Book 101 Squadron.
AIR 27/834 Operations Record Book 106 Squadron.
AIR 27/840 Operations Record Book Index 106 Squadron.
AIR 27/1046 Operations Record Book 157 Squadron.
AIR 27/1047 Operations Record Book 157 Squadron.
AIR 27/1094 Operations Record Book 169 Squadron.
AIR 27/1095 Operations Record Book 169 Squadron.
AIR 27/1456 Operations Record Book 239 Squadron.
AIR 27/1931 Operations Record Book 467 Squadron.
AIR 27/1981 Operations Record Book 515 Squadron.
AIR 27/2131 Operations Record Book 619 Squadron.
AIR 27/2148 Operations Record Book 627 Squadron.
AIR 27/2149 Operations Record Book Appendices 627 Squadron.
AIR 27/2150 Operations Record Book Appendices 627 Squadron.
AIR 27/2152 Operations Record Book 630 Squadron.
AIR 28/172 RAF Coningsby ORB 1944.
AIR 28/191 RAF Coningsby ORB Appendices 1944.
AIR 29/443/6 24 ASR Marine Unit ORB 1944.
AIR 29/680 Operations Record Book 51 OTU.
AIR 29/854 HQ ORB.
AIR 29/867 1409 Met. Flight ORB 1944.

International Bomber Command Centre Digital Archive (Lincoln University):

Audio interview with Flying Officer Ken Oatley, 627 Sqn, ref: Identifier AOatleyK170321.
Audio interview with Sgt Graham Allen, 106 Sqn, ref: Identifier AAllenG150917.
Audio interview with F/Sgt John Foster Thorp, 467 Sqn, ref: Identifier AthorpJF160412.
Audio Interview with Cpl Sheila Wilmet, Met. Office RAF Coningsby 1943.
Audio Interview with Sgt/Warrant Officer, Harry Parkins, Flight Engineer 630 Squadron 1944.
Audio Interview with F/L William Bullock, Engineering Officer RAF Coningsby 1944, ref: identifier ABullockWEJ151030, PBullockWEJ1601.
Audio Interview with Sgt, mid upper gunner, 50 Squadron, 1944, ref: identifier AWilliamsAE150608, PWilliamsAE1510.
Audio Interview with Warrant Officer Peter Stevenson, ATC RAF Syerston 1943. Ref: identifier AStevensonP160817.

Imperial War Museum Audio Archives:

Rec. of interview with Hugh Verity, 29 Sqn, ref: IWM.9939 (8/1987).
Rec. of interview with Bill Townsend, 617 Sqn, ref: IWM.8341 (10/1984).
Rec. of interview with Dave Shannon, 617 Sqn, ref: IWM.8177 (1984).
Rec. of interview with John C. Elliott, 106/617 Sqn, ref: IWM.13094 (1993).
Rec. of interview with Eileen Mary Albone, RAF Scampton driver, IWM.31697.
Rec. of interview with Lawrence W. Curtis, 617 Sqn, ref: IWM.92111.
Rec of interview with Leonard J. Sumpter, 617 Sqn, ref: IWM.7372.
Rec. of interview with Harold S. Hobday, 617 Sqn, ref: IWM.7298
Rec. of interview with Geoff King, 97 Sqn, ref: IWM.28657.

Imperial War Museum:

Flying logbook of John Hopgood.
Journal of Squadron Leader Charles Owen.
Flying logbook of Charles Owen (via his son Oliver Owen).

YouTube:

'Johnny' Johnson, 617 Sqn bomb aimer talks about Guy Gibson (2013).
BBC Documentary Dambusters Declassified (2010).

Royal Air Force Air Historical Branch:

CAS. File No. P423401/44 Excavation of Mosquito KB267/ No. 627 Sqn.

Royal Air Force Museum Hendon:

Harris Files ref: H51, H59 and file 594.
Miscellaneous Gibson papers ref: DC76/74/1324.
Guy Gibson's flying logbook.

Air Force Lists 1937-1944

Met. Office Bracknell:

Weather forecast Tuesday, 19 September 1944.

BBC Script Library:

Desert Island Disks 19 February 1944 (Guy Gibson).

Miscellaneous:

A Warrior's death (Australian flight safety) website by Robert Wilson 22/8/2022.
www.raf-pathfindersarchive.com
www.aviation-safety.net/wikibase/159154 (for 630 Squadron LE-N).

Appendix A

No. 106 Squadron Operations July 1942 – March 1943

Month	Total Sqn Raids	No. Gibson Flew	No. Gibson Flew to Germany
July 1942	9	5	4
August 1942	11	4	1
September 1942	12	3	3
October 1942	10	4	1
November 1942	10	4	0
December 1942	6	0	0
January 1943	12	2	2
February 1943	14	3	2
Up to 11 March 1943	6	1	1

Appendix B

No. 627 Squadron Target Marking Ops August-September 1944

15 August Daylight	Deelan airfield	Markers to mark aiming point with yellow TIs (4x Mosquitos with 16x yellow TIs). **N.B. This was the raid Gibson witnessed flying with SQL Ciano.**
15 August Daylight	Gilze-Rijen airfield	As above simultaneous attack.
18 August Daylight	L'Isle-Adam	PFF Mosquitos to drop Oboe TI 2 miles NE of target. Eastern target to be marked direct, western target to be marked at north and south extremities. Two markers to mark last turning point before target. (4x Mosquitos 24x 100lb and 4x 120lb smoke bombs).
25/26 August	Darmstadt	Flares and proximity blind Green TIs to be dropped by Coningsby Lancasters. 1st marker to identify target and drop Red TI, to be assessed by marker leader and if accurate, to be backed up by further Red TIs. If inaccurate, to be cancelled by a Yellow TI and remarked with further backing up if necessary. (4x Mosquitos with 4x Red TIs, 4x Yellow TIs & 4x Wanganuis
31 August Daylight	Three Flying bombs dumps	Markers to mark each of the 3 aiming points with smoke bombs.
3 September Daylight	Deelan airfield	Marker aircraft (1x Mosquito) to mark aiming point with 2x smoke bombs.

5 September Daylight	Guns to south of Brest, France	To mark 4x aiming points with TIs and smoke bombs. Reduced to just 2x aiming points before take-off. (6x Mosquitos 6x Red, 6x Green TIs).
9/10 September	Mönchengladbach	Yellow IT's followed by flares. 1st marker to identify the aiming point and drop Red TI. If accurate, to be backed up by further Red TIs. 9 Mosquitos to then drop incendiaries for main force to bomb. (4x Mosquitos with 8x Red TIs 9x Mosquitos with incendiaries).
11/12 September	Darmstadt	Green proximity markers to be dropped followed by flares. Marking to be assessed and a Red TI dropped. If TI accurate, to be backed up by remaining Red TIs and Red spot flares. (6x Mosquitos with 10x Red TIs, 2x Red spot flares & 7x Mosquitos with incendiaries).
12/13 September	Stuttgart	Flares and proximity Green markers to be dropped by Lancasters. 1st marker to identify aiming point and to drop Red TI or Red spot flare. Results to be assessed by marker leader and passed to controller. If accurate to be backed up by as many remaining markers as marker leader considers necessary. (6x Mosquitos with Red spot flares/Red TIs, 7x Mosquitos with incendiaries).
18/19 September	Bremerhaven	Blind Green proximity markers to be dropped followed by flares. 1st marker to identify aiming point to drop a Red TI. To be assessed by marker leader and if accurate to be backed up by remaining markers. Assessment to be passed to controller. If impossible to mark, markers to backup original blind proximity markers. (6x Mosquitos with 14x Red TIs).

Appendix C

Known Operations/Flights of No. 627 Squadron Mosquitos KB213 & KB267

June-September 1944:

N.B. KB267 was the Mosquito Gibson was flying on 19 September 1944.

Date/Target	Aircraft	Aircrew	Comments
27 June / Vitry	KB213	Wg Cdr Fg Off Dally	Marker 1 Markers dropped
7 July / St. Leu d'Esserent	KB213	Fg Off Boothright Fg Off Holdaway	lx Yellow TI Hung-up
20 July / Courtrai	KB213	Fg Off Whitehead Sgt Watt	Dropped TIs in dive
26 July / Givors	KB267	Flt Lt Bray Fl Sgt Swales	Starboard engine failed, return to base with all TIs on board
9 August / La Pallice	KB267	Flt Lt Reid Fg Off Ward	Dive bombed target
	KB213	Plt Off Boyden Flt Sgt Fenwick	As above
15 August / Deelan AF	KB267	Flt Lt Oakley Fg Off Crombie	TI Hung-up N.B. This was the raid Gibson accompanied in P38
18 August / Forêt de L'Isle-Adam	KB267	Fg Off Thomson Fg Off Harris	Dropped TIs

Date/Target	Aircraft	Aircrew	Comments
6 September	KB213	Sqn Ldr Owen Air Cdre Cousins	Local flight
7 September Dive	KB213	Sqn Ldr Owen Flt Lt Bowes	Bombing practice
10 September / Mönchengladbach	KB267	Fg Off Boothright Flt Sgt Clarke	Dive bombed target
	KB213	Sqn Ldr Owen Flt Lt Bowes	Controller
11 September / Darmstadt	KB267	Fg Off Brown Flt Lt Cowan	Dropped incendiaries
11 September	KB213	Sqn Ldr Owen Wg Cdr Simpson	Local flight
12 September / Stuttgart	KB276 (typo read KB267)	Fg Off Brown Flt Lt Cowan	Dropped incendiaries
	KB213	Sqn Ldr Owen Flt Lt Bowes	Controller
19 September / Rheydt Mönchengladbach	KB276	Wg Cdr Gibson Sqn Ldr Warwick	1x TI Hung-up?

Appendix D

Gibson's Timeline on 19 September 1944

Time	Details
Morning	Night flying test at RAF Coningsby of Mosquito which was declared unserviceable. Request made for a No. 627 Squadron Mosquito to be made available that night.
Lunchtime	Lunch taken in the Officers' Mess at Coningsby with No. 97 Squadron crew.
Early afternoon	Dai Thomas the navigator from No. 627 Squadron said to have been his deputed navigator reported sick with a head cold.
Mid-afternoon	Bremerhaven raid cancelled and new raid on Rheydt and Mönchengladbach planned by No. 5 Group HQ.
	Gibson telephoned by Eve. She later recalled he was irritated.
	Other navigators made themselves absent before James Warwick deputed to be Gibson's navigator.
	Gibson briefed by Charles Owen on raid.
17:45hrs	Briefings for raid take place across No. 5 Group during which Gibson is named as Controller.
18:30hrs	Gibson and Warwick driven to Woodhall Spa to collect spare Mosquito KB213. Upon arrival Gibson discards aircraft and a disagreement ensues before he takes another aircraft.
19:00-19:30hrs	Warwick is briefed in the cockpit by an engineering officer before Gibson tells him to get out.
19:51hrs	Gibson and Warwick take-off from Woodhall Spa.
21:35-22:00hrs	Gibson and Warwick over target.
22:30hrs	Gibson and Warwick crash at Steenbergen.

Index

Other books by M.S. Morgan and published by Pen & Sword:

The Hurricane Pilot Who Became a Gestapo Agent.

Hitler's RAF Collaborators.

The Death of Prince George, The Duke of Kent 1942.
A New Investigation to Find the Truth. (Due Autumn 2024)

Author's website: msmorganbooks.co.uk